## Praise for *Pick Money*

"*Pick Money* breaks down what it really takes to build a major success. In this book, Shawn shares the tools he used and the mindset he followed to pave his way to the top. If you're dreaming of success, *Pick Money* gives you the road map to get there."

—Barbara Corcoran, star of ABC's *Shark Tank*

"Shawn's philosophy fuses the no-nonsense leadership of a football coach with the sharp instincts of an entrepreneur. In a ruthless business climate, his fresh perspective is both rare and essential."

—Patrick Bet-David, Owner, New York Yankees, and Founder, Valuetainment and PHP Agency

"First and foremost, Shawn is that dude. He is him. Period. The end. Knowing his story and background, he's not just talking the talk—he's walking that walk and doing his thang throughout the process. He speaks the truth and real life experience. If you're looking to take your life to the next level and own your own, this is the book for you. In this book Shawn is like that boxing coach in the corner telling you to throw that left, right, hook . . . he's *your* coach, your navigational system along your journey to help you break those barriers and take you and your family to places you may have never dreamt before."

—"Coach Prime" Deion Sanders, *New York Times* Bestselling Author, *Elevate and Dominate*

"*Pick Money* is your blueprint to financial independence and freedom! It lays out for you what's important, why it's important, what to avoid, and the best practices you need to make more money. Lots of it. You won't find fluffy non-sense or theories, but an immersion into real strategies based on successes of real people making REAL money."

—Dave Anderson, CEO, Learn To Lead, and Author, *Elevate Your Excellence*

# PICK
# MONEY

# PICK MONEY

## FIVE YEARS TO FINANCIAL FREEDOM

**SHAWN MEAIKE**

MATT HOLT

Matt Holt Books
An Imprint of BenBella Books, Inc.
Dallas, TX

MATT HOLT BENBELLA

Matt Holt is an imprint of BenBella Books, Inc.
8080 N. Central Expressway
Suite 1700
Dallas, TX 75206
benbellabooks.com
Send feedback to feedback@benbellabooks.com



Printed in the United States of America
10 9 8 7 6 5 4 3 2 1

Library of Congress Control Number: 2026000724
ISBN 9781637749203 (hardcover)
ISBN 9781637749210 (electronic)

Editing by Greg Brown
Copyediting by Michael Fedison
Proofreading by Jenny Bridges and Denise Pangia
Text design and composition by PerfecType, Nashville, TN
Cover design by Rachael Brandenburg
Cover image © Adobe Stock / Megane
Printed by Lake Book Manufacturing

# CONTENTS

# CHAPTER 1

# PICK MONEY OR STAY BROKE

The first time I realized I had to pick money, I was thinking about tucking a couple of cans of expensive baby formula under my jacket and walking out the door of the supermarket, hoping I wouldn't get caught.

By the time my new son was just a few days old, my wife—later to become my ex-wife—had already discovered that he just wasn't taking to breastfeeding, even though she'd had no trouble breastfeeding our daughter.

The pediatrician told us our son had a sensitivity to milk, and we would need to find a formula that he could digest. We went through three or four different formulas—soy-based, this-based, that-based—but he struggled with all of them. It seemed like he just wasn't willing to drink anything, and we were really worried.

A different pediatrician told us there was one more option, a very expensive formula called Alimentum. And she gave us two cans so we could try it.

The Alimentum felt like a miracle. He loved it, taking right to it and then going to sleep. He was happy and fed, and we were ecstatic.

Jump forward a couple of days. We're almost out of formula, so I have to go to the store to get some more. I figured, hell, it can't be that much. But when I got there, it was *so* expensive. It was like 30 or 40 bucks a can. And it wasn't covered by insurance, even though we had good insurance. And here I was thinking about how our son would be going through one of these cans every two days. This was going to cost us close to 200 bucks a month.

That day at the supermarket is one I'll never forget. I'd worked at my real estate job all day long, running around trying to make some money. But I never made enough, even though I was also working a second job. We had so many bills, but my wife wasn't working at the time, and it was beyond tight on only my income. Meanwhile, my mother-in-law was dying, and my father-in-law needed to move in with us. Now I was going to have to work even harder to make enough to feed this kid his damn Alimentum.

I'm looking at the store and thinking, there's no security at all. I don't steal from anybody. I don't steal, period. But Stop & Shop seemed to be doing good. If I walked out that door with four or five cans of formula, I could save myself a couple of hundred bucks, probably without hurting them at all.

I didn't steal that day. But I'll never forget that feeling, the way I rationalized it, and how close I came to becoming a thief . . . of baby formula of all things. The fact that *stealing* seemed like a good idea for a minute really put a spotlight on how bad things were.

I don't come from money. There wasn't anybody to help me if I couldn't pay my bills. I never had one single person I could call to help out. My mother didn't have it. There wasn't anybody else in my family who had it or would give it to me. And even if there was someone to ask, I never would—because I didn't believe it was anyone else's responsibility but my own.

Growing up, I saw how, no matter how hard my mother worked, there was never enough money. Now I was repeating that pattern, and I realized something had to change. I swore to myself, I would never be in a situation where I couldn't provide my family with the necessities of life. Ever.

As I dug my wallet out and paid for fancy formula I really couldn't afford, I realized that day that I needed to make a decision—to start picking money, so I would never again feel I couldn't afford something for my child. That decision changed my and my family's life. Forever.

People hear me say "pick money," and they think it sounds cold, or a little evil. Like I have misplaced priorities. That's because people are largely taught to never pick money. Most people will absolutely never pick money. And those people always wind up working for the people who do pick money.

Most people stumble through life without focusing on money at all. They talk about wanting to have a better life for their family. They talk about not wanting to worry about money. They talk about a legacy. But they never pick money, even though money is the best way to achieve all those things.

When I decided to pick money, everything changed.

## PICK MONEY, NOT BUSY

I sat down that night when everybody was sleeping.

I decided that everything moving forward in my life would take a back seat to me picking money. And I started writing out the things in my life that I was doing that didn't help me pick money.

I was still there for my kids. I was still laser-focused on my faith and my family. But I knew that I was finally done complaining. I would no longer have a broke mindset, a broke mentality, and a broke lifestyle. Beyond focusing on picking money, I started doing the work to feel that making that choice, picking money, wasn't slimy, evil, cold, or self-serving—it was completely okay.

That night, I came to my second powerful realization. I saw that I had been picking busy instead of picking money. At the time, I was working two full-time jobs—40 hours a week as a social worker at the Department of Children and Families in Connecticut on top of 40 hours a week as a real estate broker. Plus, I was doing anything else that would make me some money. If somebody called me and said they had 41 units in their apartment building that they needed tenants for, I'd say, "Okay, if I can get it to 75 percent occupancy within thirty days, you pay me X, Y, Z."

My head was on a swivel, always looking for other things to do to make money.

I was doing all this on two to four hours of sleep every night. And I was doubling down on one of life's biggest lies: that all this hard work would result in financial success.

I watched a lot of busy people, and I assumed that they were successful. I assumed that if you were working hard, well, hell, you must be doing well. But I was wrong.

I started looking at my own schedule. I thought to myself, *You work hard, but you're still worried about money. You're scared about all the people you need to take care of now.*

I started looking at what I was doing in the real estate business. I looked at the open houses I was attending. All the floor duty I was doing at the office. All the phones I was answering. All without any consistent guarantee of making money on commissions.

For the first couple of months, I blindly did what the company asked me to do. I worked hard to keep the clients happy.

And I noticed that most agents were not in control of the dynamic. It was the clients who were in charge.

And they were in charge of me too. For one example, there was a guy named Craig. He and his wife wanted to look at homes. They'd never purchased a home before, but they were prequalified, which means a lender had written them a prequalification letter that indicated they were in a financial situation where they could choose to buy a house.

Over the next three weeks, I took them to see maybe 30, 35 houses. That's no exaggeration, and it's not even unusual.

And finally, at the end of those three weeks, while I was showing them *another* house, it hit me. These two had no desire to *actually buy* anything.

This kind of thing happens often. When you have a couple who are house hunting, sometimes one of them isn't really ready to buy. Or one of them wants the perfect home. Or they have unrealistic expectations that can never be met, like wanting to pay three hundred grand for a house that's worth half a million dollars or wanting an absolutely perfect house that doesn't have a single problem of any kind.

That day, while Craig's wife was in another room, I said, "Craig, do you mind if I ask you a question? You can be honest with me. Y'all are never going to buy a mother-freaking house, are you? You ain't going to buy shit. Right?"

And he looked me dead in the eyes and said, "Bro, I don't know that we're really ready. She wants to buy a house. But I don't know."

So I told him I was going to help him out. And when his wife came in, I said, "Hey, we just talked. He's not ready. He's uncomfortable. You two need to talk, because he's terrified to buy a house. He doesn't think you're in a good enough financial position for it. And if one of you wants it, and one of you doesn't, well, I'm not a marriage counselor, but that's going to work out really poorly for you. So I'm not showing you any more houses. Our relationship is over. Good luck to you both."

Spending weeks satisfying the whims of a client and maybe getting the sale and maybe not just goes with the territory for a lot of real estate agents. But if you ever watch the top salespeople, you'll see that they seem to take control of their situation.

That's what I saw the top sales guy in my office was doing. He had a different way of approaching things. So, after I'd been in the office a couple of months, I asked him, "What is the number one mistake everybody in here is making?" And he said, "Their clients lead them around, as opposed to the other way around."

When I asked him how he changed that, he said, "I take control. I let my clients know that I'm busy. I'm not here to entertain them. And I only deal with people that have real buying potential."

He never would have touched Craig and his wife. Let alone spent three weeks letting them run him all over town.

So how could I start changing my philosophy and my strategy? My manager wasn't any good, and the other people around me weren't really any good, so they couldn't help me find a better approach. The top salesman was really good, but he generally didn't talk to anybody. He was a mean old man who stayed apart from the rest of us. I was surprised he'd told me anything. I think he just appreciated my having the courage to talk to him. But he wasn't going to mentor me, so I needed to figure things out for myself.

I started really thinking about my business and what I was doing wrong. I thought about all the people like Craig, and of all the times I'd shown people house after house without knowing if they were going to buy *any* of them.

Then I had a thought: If I sent people all the listings for the houses I'm working to sell, how many top choices could they really have? If they have more than three that they want me to drive them around to, then they're probably trying to entertain themselves. A couple is bored, so the wife says, "Let's do something this Saturday." And the husband says, "Hey, let's go look at houses all day."

I wasn't going to participate in that anymore. So I made a change. I would show people three houses. I would say to the clients, "Listen, I'm going to send you all the information about all these houses. You drive by them at your leisure because I'm too busy negotiating deals, helping clients get the best house. I don't have time to do the taxiing. You do that. Once you narrow it to three, I'm your guy."

I also decided I wouldn't show them properties at all unless they had a letter. Not a prequalification letter that your cousin sent from the mortgage company. But a letter that I could validate stating that they had the ability to buy a property at a specific price.

And I told them, "I'm a ridiculously good negotiator. So I'm going to get you what you need."

I was setting limits while also selling them on my services.

That didn't mean I would *never* show people a fourth house if they had genuine reasons why they didn't want the first three. The roof leaks in this one, and I don't want to fix it. I didn't realize how much traffic was on the street of this one. That kind of stuff. Those were fair points that deserved to be heard.

Setting that limit just blew my business up. It repelled all the people who wanted to waste my time, but people who were willing to narrow it down to three houses—instead of having an all-day, chauffeured tour of the neighborhood—those were the people who were worth my time.

As for Craig, you know what? A year later, he called me. He was like, "Hey, man, what are you doing?" I was like, "Still in real estate. What are you up to?" He said, "Dude, I'm ready. As a matter of fact, I already know what I want to buy. Can you take us to look at it?"

I showed him the house. We're there for probably 15 minutes. I made an offer that day. It got accepted. The sale closed in a month and a half. And I got paid.

Instead of being mad that I'd cut them off a year earlier, Craig and his wife wanted to come back to me. Craig said, "I knew you wouldn't lie to us. You'd be direct."

And after seeing how well my three-houses policy was working, I said to myself, "Why don't I just carry myself like this in business always?" I want to attract all the people who are actually serious about doing business, and I want to repel all the people who are a waste of my freaking time. So I need to do everything based on that strategy going forward.

## MORE STRATEGY MEANS LESS WORK

I started picking money over picking busy. Everybody around me thought my real estate policies were odd things to put in place, but when I did, my business started to flourish.

Once I discovered the secret of picking money over busy, I started doing that everywhere. I used that same strategy of setting rules that would create success without a lot of running around for investing in real estate.

I had already bought some real estate—I was just investing in rentals at the time. And I decided to become a guy who was going to be scarce with his time, but able to make a deal quickly. I wasn't going to go look at five properties a day, or twelve properties a week. I was going to find one or two that made sense for me and put all my time into those. I was done with doing anything that wasted my time.

So I broke down exactly what I wanted in a property.

There were two large casinos in southeastern Connecticut. They were big, and they were the biggest employers in the area at that time.

So my first decision was, I'll only buy properties that are on the bus route to those casinos. So if you don't have a car, you're good. And if you do have a car, you're also good.

Then I looked at those properties in areas that fit that criteria. And I started evaluating them on safety—what areas would cause me trouble and what areas wouldn't. Because I didn't want to collect rent with a gun. I've always carried a gun, and I can protect myself. But in a neighborhood where the guys and girls carry guns, too, and engage in significant criminal activity, they aren't going to give a shit about my gun—or about paying me rent. And I'm not going to argue with them. I spent a lot of time in bad neighborhoods when I was a kid, and I knew enough to stay out of them.

I'd narrowed my options down to properties in decent neighborhoods that were near the casinos and on the bus route. The next step was to think about the limits on what properties to buy in those areas.

First, I would never buy a single- or two-family. There wasn't enough money in it. And if it was a property with six or more units, you couldn't get regular loans for it. Only commercial loans, which weren't good for me. So I was now only looking for three-, four-, and five-family units in decent neighborhoods along that specific bus route.

The funnel was getting tight. Maybe I'd have 10 properties that fit that criteria. I could start looking at getting the best return on my dollar. If a property was overpriced relative to its appraised value, that was a no. If your house is worth $300 grand and you put it up at $420, you're a dumbass. And I don't negotiate with dumbasses. If it's worth $300 and you put it on at $305, you ain't stupid, and I'll talk to you.

Once I cut out the overpriced properties, I'd wind up with four or five that were worth considering. At this point, I would call up a guy who worked for me and ask him to drive by them and tell me about the neighbors. What do they look like? Drive by at midnight on a Friday or Saturday. Look to see if there are like four cars in a drive where they're all raising hell. You don't want that.

So, after those drive-bys, I'd be down to maybe one or two properties that I was seriously considering.

While I was setting and working my limits, other investors were just shot-gunning it, looking at everything all the time. I think a lot of them were looking for something they could feel they really stole. They wanted to find the too-good-to-be-true deal. They wanted to be the winner. They'd go into a bad neighborhood because a property was selling under the appraised value, and they'd think they'd found a great deal.

But I just liked mundane, simple, boring, and profitable. Nothing flashy. Nothing risky. A total cookie-cutter approach.

Of course, I wasn't this singular genius who had come up with a system that no one else had. There were other people who wanted the same properties I was going for. But I also had cash. I could go in and say, "Here's the deal, bro. I'll pay you cash, right now. Let's get it done."

Another selling point for me was that I never did inspections. A 20-minute walkthrough was enough for me. I'd walk through the house, see if there was any water damage, check if the roof was leaking, make sure all the faucets turned on, see where I'd have to put in some money. But there was no detailed inspection that someone else might use to negotiate the price.

Someone might have wanted 288K. I'd offer 260 cash, as is. No mortgage, no inspection. All I needed was a clear title, and I was good. The seller got to walk away and never think about the place again.

There are risks to handling things this way. I've gone in after I bought a property and let the water run for 30 minutes and realized it did leak after all. And no matter how carefully you try to select a neighborhood where there's not a lot of trouble, sometimes the trouble comes anyway. Once, I bought a house in a neighborhood where there'd never been a drive-by shooting. And the next day there was a drive-by shooting where the house had 18 or 19 rounds fired into it. Everyone in the neighborhood was shocked.

Another time I bought two five-family units located next to each other with a connecting roof, rented them out, and a cop called me. He said, "Hey, dude, you know these guys you rented to are like separate gangs, right?" I was like, "Are they pretend gangs or real gangs?" He said, "No, I think they're real gangs."

Even though I was trying to avoid really bad neighborhoods, these weren't wealthy suburbs, so you had to be prepared to deal with problems when they came up.

I bought a property in Norwich, sight unseen. I called the people up, asked, "What do you want for it?" They told me. I said, "What kind of condition is it?" They said, "No one lives there legally, but we've had squatters, so you can imagine."

I made them a cash offer of $60,000 for a two-family house. They accepted it. We closed it. Title in a week and done.

The old owners said they'd done everything to get the squatters out. But they were still breaking in at night. So, when me and my buddy went out to the property to check it out around 9 PM, I brought a gun. And I banged on the door to warn anyone there to get out.

The place was disgusting. But that's what I'd expected based on what I'd paid for it.

When we got upstairs, I could hear dogs barking, left behind by the squatters.

When I opened a door a little bit, a couple of big pit bulls came charging. I slammed the door as fast as you've ever shut a door in your life.

So I had hungry, angry pit bulls in my house. You can't just shoo them out the door and hope a neighbor adopts them. I called 911 and animal control came and took them away.

So, there were risks. But most of the time those risks paid off. Because I'd built relationships over the years with so many realtors and so many people in the area, the price was usually fair, and the deals usually easy to navigate.

And the price should be fair. For me, that's the rule in business. A good deal is good for both parties. If you don't do deals where both sides win, you will not do many deals, so picking money means making fair deals. Not chasing things at crazy low prices and feeling like you're getting a steal or pulling one over on someone. That's the broke way of doing it—"Hey, I got it for this much; it was a steal." But stealing doesn't make realtors want to do more business with you. And sometimes people who think they're getting a steal are actually buying a headache.

I'm a businessman. I'll pay what's fair. That's all part of picking money.

## CRACKING THE SUCCESS CODE

As I found strategies to pull in money without running around 24/7 like a madman, I was thinking more and more about the keys to becoming a successful businessman. What's the secret? I wondered. I had gone all in on picking money, and now I was dreaming about creating a passive cash flow that could set my lifestyle free.

It all came down to building a business where picking money would eventually lead to a time when I could enjoy my family and my life while the money steadily flowed in. I wanted an income that wasn't contingent on what I sold and what I did that day. I dreamed about a different lifestyle with a lot more freedom.

I started to watch people who were businessmen. Businessmen in real estate, transportation, at UPS. I observed what they were doing as well as what they didn't bother doing.

I became a student. If you were a successful businessperson, I observed you, read about you, or watched you on TV or social media. It was just like I was watching game film when I played sports. I'm like, "All right, he does that. I like that." I watched businessmen interact in their environment, and I picked something up from all of them.

I watched how they communicated, how they accessed financing, how they built relationships, how they looked at the projects they became involved in, and how they managed their employees. I watched how they talked with their friends, how they treated people in restaurants, and just how they lived their lives in general.

I learned public speaking by watching people control the stage. Did they interact with the crowd? Were they trying to be funny? Educational? Did they take questions from the stage?

I learned sales by watching their posture, seeing the way they matched people's tonality when they were talking to them. I saw how presumptive they were, directing the conversation by saying, "Here's what we're gonna do," when it was really, "I'm telling you what to do."

Whatever the industry—real estate, life insurance, waste management transportation, delivery—the principles were the same. Because they are universal.

- → **Work Ethic:** I saw that these successful businessmen had a greater work ethic than the people around them.
- → **Communication:** I saw they could effectively communicate with everybody, at every level of their company.
- → **Hands-on:** They delegated what they needed to, but these men were hands-on—they took ownership of their business.
- → **Humility:** While they had a lot of success, the ones I was studying weren't egotistical. They continued to grow and scale and move up, always keeping some semblance of humility.
- → **Mentoring:** I saw that they were trying to help other people, inside and outside their company, get to where they were. They weren't along for the ride by themselves—they wanted to bring people with them.
- → **Decisive:** They made decisions quickly in a crisis. When things were going well, it was a democracy—everybody was involved. But when the shit hit the fan, it was a dictatorship until things got back on track.

Watching these successful people, I realized that I was only pretending to be a businessman. I had an LLC, real estate investments, and property management, but I was just a poseur. I couldn't tell you what my net income was or tell you my bottom line. I never thought about any of that because I wasn't picking money. I was picking busy. I was picking what I assumed everybody else was doing.

I was picking being a "businessman." Being in charge of a business. Having X number of LLCs. Doing X number of transactions. Making a couple of dollars. But I wasn't doing what those successful businessmen were doing at all.

I'd become obsessed with picking money. For me and, most importantly, for my family.

When I talk about picking money, sometimes people will say, "I will never pick money over my family." But that's a weak, pathetic excuse. I was picking money *for* my family. I was picking money because I wanted my family to have a better life.

And it's not just about picking money for my family. I pick money to give back to my community. It's great to be the guy who volunteers his time to do something like build a playground. But the guy who makes the biggest difference is the one who donates a million bucks for the land and the equipment. Without that, there are just 30 people sitting around a vacant piece of property, looking at each other.

I want to go out and make the money to give those 30 people something to build. I'll come out and be the thirty-first person as well, working side by side with them, but I'd rather pick having the money to make it happen. That has the biggest impact.

That's what this book is about. Not just making money but making the kind of money that lets you change lives—starting with your own. The businesspeople I met weren't smarter than everyone else. They weren't luckier. They just made different choices. And in the pages ahead, I'm going to show you exactly what those choices are so you can start making them too.

→CHAPTER 1←

# REFLECTION QUESTIONS

1. Your Baby Formula Moment: When was the last time money stress forced you into a corner? Write down that specific moment.

2. Name Your Why: What would financial freedom actually give you? Don't say something vague like "security"—what exact situation would change?

3. The Mirror Test: Can you look at yourself right now and say you're doing everything possible to pick money? If not, what's stopping you?

CHAPTER 2

# PICK MINDSET

## *SIX STEPS TO FINANCIAL FREEDOM*

The sad truth is that most people will never pick money—not because they can't, but because they choose not to. I knew a guy who worked eight to three, Monday through Friday, for 30 years at the same company. Never worked any extra hours, never looked for another job. And anytime his family needed anything at all, he was asking us for it. Can you donate to this? Can you pay for my daughter's whatever so she can play on this team?

And when anyone else in his community needed something, it was always, "I ain't got nothing to give."

He was doing a job he could do in his sleep because he was picking comfort. He hung out when he wanted, drank when he wanted, watched TV when he wanted, and asked other people to pick up the slack.

Meanwhile, I'm getting up at five and going to bed at one, six days a week for my family. I'm like, "I'll donate money to the homeless shelter, I'll donate money to people who have no money, but I'm not going to give you money so your kids can do extracurricular things because you want to choose comfort over your family. It's not my responsibility to help you, bro. Get a second job. Get a better job. Dude, you have children. Go out there and figure it out."

So many people pick comfort over money. They pick approval. They pick excuses for why they aren't doing things. They pick negativity so they can keep complaining when life doesn't go their way. They pick a lack of accountability.

They can pick whatever they want. I picked money.

When you pick money, people might judge you, might give you advice about how you should be doing this and not that. If they do, just look them in the eyes and say, "Stop assuming I want your life or your advice when you have no idea what I'm going through."

Protect your mindset. Don't pretend, or posture, or play the poseur. Just do the best you can.

I believe that, ultimately, I'll be judged by God—in fact, I'm 100% sure of that, and it weighs on me. But the judgment of people means nothing. Don't let it stop you. Pick what you want.

## PICKING MONEY, STEP BY STEP

Once I picked money, I became goal-oriented.

I asked myself, "How do I raise my income by 20% a year, every year?" I wasn't trying to leap from $80,000 or $100,000 a year to five million overnight. If I'm making $100,000 now, how do I make $120,000 next year?

That part wasn't complicated. Eventually, I got to two hundred grand. Then it became, "How do I make 240 next year? What does it look like when I hit a million?" I was moving up in increments, but I never believed there was a cap.

The same thing goes for building the mindset. You don't get there overnight. You need to create a system—clear steps you can come back to again and again—so you don't slip back into picking comfort, excuses, or approval instead of money.

In this chapter, I'm going to take you through six steps that form the foundation for picking money. Think of them as a reset button: Whenever you feel yourself drifting back into old habits, revisit these steps to get back on track.

## STEP ONE: FIND YOUR IMPEDIMENT

What is your impediment? You probably have one. Is it drinking? Getting high? Gambling? No work ethic? People in your life you can't offend—or can't say no to? Cigarettes? Lying to yourself? Overeating? Making excuses? Being too critical of yourself? Doubt? Negative self-talk? Worrying what people think?

What's holding you back?

Back when I first decided to pick money, one of my biggest impediments was busyness. I thought being the hardest worker in the room would guarantee success, so I worked two full-time jobs, chased side hustles, and ran on two to four hours of sleep. But all that busy work wasn't moving me forward. It just left me exhausted.

I had to realize that being busy wasn't the same as picking money. Until I admitted that, I couldn't make real progress.

If you want to pick money, you have to identify your own impediment and deal with it now. Otherwise, you'll keep spinning your wheels, working hard while never getting ahead.

## STEP TWO: FIND SOMEONE WHO WILL TELL YOU THE TRUTH

The first decision I made before having kids—one that didn't really benefit me financially until I picked money—was getting sober.

I stopped drinking and using drugs because I was a menace. I was dangerous. I'd jump off roofs into cars. I'd fight guys anywhere, anytime, for no reason at all. I made bad decisions. At the time, I didn't see how that was holding me back.

This was when I was working at the State of Connecticut Department of Children and Families as a social worker. There was a guy quite a bit older than me named Mike.

I respected Mike. He was a supervisor before I became one. A guy's guy, easy to talk to.

One day he told me, "They're never going to promote you here or take you seriously if you keep drinking and partying the way you do."

At first I thought, *That's odd. I show up. I stay busy. I take all the overtime they ask for. I'm 20 now, and in a few years, I should be successful in this job. What does it matter if I get drunk every night?* But Mike said, "People respect the work you do, but if you don't stop partying, it won't matter."

Then he hit me with a question I couldn't recover from: "When you have kids one day, and they need something from you but you're under the influence, what's going to happen? If you can't help your kids because you're drunk, who will? Before you bring kids into the world, think about that first."

I could have said, "Screw you, Mike." But I didn't. I respected him more than anybody there because he was always honest with me.

That's what Step Two is about. You have to find your Mike. Someone who cares enough about you to be honest, even when it's uncomfortable. Someone who doesn't have a vested interest in anything except seeing you succeed. Someone who won't pick their own comfort over telling you the truth.

If you don't have that person yet, go find them. They may not be in your life right now, but they're out there. And until you have someone willing to point out your blind spots, those blind spots will run your life.

You need to take a hard look at your impediments and what you'll need to overcome to pick money. Then create your success plan—how you'll grow 20% a year. Start with the mindset that you're picking money not just for yourself but for your family, your community, and your future success.

Getting sober wasn't instant. The first year was awful. The second year was less awful. But after 24 months, sobriety started to feel true to who I was day to day. If I hadn't developed the ability to be sober, I never could have picked money successfully.

I'm not telling you that everybody needs to stop drinking or using drugs. What I am telling you is this: If you're putting something in your body that poisons you—mentally or physically—stop. You'll give yourself a better chance to succeed.

Now, some people can't just stop. If you're an addict who gets up in the morning and can't function until you've had a drink, then I'm not talking to you right now. You need to go to AA, go to rehab, get a therapist. I've lived that way, and it's a hard existence. You need to make recovery your focus.

But many who drink way too much aren't alcoholics. They just choose to drink—to relax, or because their friends do, or because they're bored. They could stop tomorrow, but they just don't want to, because they're addicted to comfort.

When I talk about sobriety, most people are like, "I just don't know how to do it. When I go out, I drink just to fit in." And that's just sad.

People keep negative things in their lives because they're comfortable, or because they believe it's the only way to have fun. "I don't have fun unless I'm drinking. I don't have fun unless I'm getting high."

But your impediment may not be too much drinking or too many drugs. It might just be complacency.

I heard the legendary football coach Nick Saban talk about how abnormal it is for people to achieve something and still want it as badly as they did before they achieved it. He said a kid might make an A, then take two weeks off from studying and make a C. So they end up a B student—because after they made an A, they couldn't keep grinding.

It's normal to get comfortable. It's really hard to keep grinding once you've hit your goal. Then you're like, "I'm good. I've got my championship ring—why would I want another?"

Maybe your impediment is who you're listening to. Whose voice do you hear most? Is it your own? And if it's yours, is it even qualified to tell you what to do? Or are you your own impediment?

Maybe it's other people. Maybe your inability to cut certain people out of your life is the impediment.

Some people are addicted to drama. They don't feel comfortable unless they're talking shit about others. When I was working jobs, if someone said, "You know what sucks about Tim?" I'd call out, "Hold on a minute. Hey, Tim, come here. Tom doesn't like you. Tom, tell Tim what you don't like about him." Then I'd sit there, drink my Diet Mountain Dew, and watch them.

Because I don't have time for that. I'm not playing your negative game.

Broke people love negativity. When I was growing up, every TV in my apartment building had Jerry Springer or Maury Povich on. Broke people love drama because they want to see other people's lives fucked up. It makes them feel better about their own fucked-up lives.

I don't like any of that. Why should I take pleasure in someone else's pain? Why should I want their lives to be messed up? Why should I watch a car crash in real life?

So, when you're looking at your impediments, ask yourself: "Am I seeking comfort?" Because I promise you, short-term comfort will bring long-term discomfort.

When you clear out the things holding you back, you can take that focus and put it on picking money. Then you can achieve anything.

So write down your impediments—the negative things you know you need to stop doing. And if you only come up with one or two, you're lying to yourself.

Here's a great question to ask in any situation: Whether you're hanging around certain people, still talking to negative voices, still partying, gambling all your money away, or making stupid purchases, ask—"What good comes out of this?" If the only good is a quick rush or a short hit of justification, it won't help you in the long run.

Creating this mindset has to become your mission. That way, nobody can mess with it.

Now, nobody can mess with my mindset. Because in the future, I don't want my kids—or anyone who relies on me—making decisions based on money. If I don't pick money, I'll never get them there. The mindset becomes the mission. You 100% can do this.

## STEP THREE: DEFAULT TO WORK

Figuring out your impediments is crucial because it means figuring out *what's* keeping you from working hard. The rub is that sometimes doubling down and working hard is the only way to push past those same impediments that stop you from working.

I've found the way through that contradiction is to learn to default to work, automatically putting yourself in the space where picking money is possible at least. If you can default to work, you can change everything. Feeling depressed? Then go to work. Drinking too much? Go to work, and you'll have less time for that. It won't make your problems go away. It's not your long-term solution. But if you have a bunch of bad shit going on in your life, and you handle one thing well, becoming successful at it, well, the bad shit's still there, but what's weird is, it's not as bad. You start to come out the other side. You start to think, *Now what? My marriage failed. I drink too much. I'm not happy. I had a bad childhood. None of that has changed. But I'm having success in this other part of my life. I've got a win.*

People have told me that everybody can't have the mindset that I have. That's a lie. I don't have some super brain, some special DNA, some secret potion. I'm not special. There's nothing I can do that you can't do if you choose to. The lie of capitalism is that people are rich because they're special. They are not any more special than you. But they might be working harder.

Think about your work ethic. Honestly. How strong is it? Chances are not as solid as you might imagine. For a lot of people, one of their biggest impediments is a terrible work ethic. They are just unwilling to work hard.

And I get it. Working hard sucks, especially when no matter how hard you work, you never get out of the hole you're in. Others don't put in enough effort because they just don't know how to work hard, or even what that really means.

Some people work hard only when things are going well. As long as there's no impediment, they'll clock in and do their thing. But give them a bad hour, a rough day, or a tough week, and they give up. They stop grinding.

The real test is how you respond when you're down. When people are pulling against you. When you're worried about being seen as a failure. That's where the rubber meets the road. How are you then? Do you keep working—or do you quit?

The reason I've been able to pick money in every environment is that I never gave a shit about circumstances. Whether things were good or bad, you just do what you can do that day. You have to just commit to never stopping, even when you feel there's no point. Just say, "I will never stop."

When I picked money, I knew I couldn't get complacent. It didn't matter how much success I had—I was going to keep grinding. Because I respect momentum.

People say to me, "You're still grinding. It's uncivilized how much you want to grow and how much you never let up." And I say, "Thank you." Because, to me, that's a compliment. And because I want to show people how to pick money and thrive.

## STEP FOUR: WORK CRAZY HARD NOW SO YOU CAN WORK SMART LATER

The goal, if you're looking to pick money, is to find a way to become financially free as soon as possible. Even though I'm still grinding, I'm not grinding 24/7 the way I used to. What I mean by financially free is getting to a place where you're able to survive and where you have passive income to rely on.

That income might be fully passive—investments, the stock market, whatever you're building—or it might mean you've taken your active income and learned to work smarter. Maybe you go from selling 7 days a week, 12 hours a day, to 40 hours on your own schedule. Or maybe you get so good you can pull in the same income in 20 hours.

The point is to get to where you're not working constantly. But that doesn't happen overnight. At the start, everybody who gets into business has to work harder than they ever have before. Whether that means six months, a year, or five years depends on your market, your skill, and how well you leverage yourself and negotiate.

In real estate, I worked seven days a week for about six months. After a year, I was delegating. After 18 months, my income was 100% passive.

I taught my guy to do everything. I'd still look at new properties in the morning, but otherwise I was free to move on to other things. In the waste management business, it was passive from day one—but only because I had enough capital to put in up front.

That's the trade-off. When you start something that doesn't take much capital, your sweat equity is the capital. If you step into an industry that takes five or seven or ten million dollars just to get in, you probably won't be the one working—you already bought the inventory.

So how hard and how long you work depends on what you've chosen and how fast you can grow in that space. Later in this book, I'll show you how to create a plan and track your progress so you'll know when to keep pushing and when to start easing off.

One of your goals should be not to make the mistake I made. Early on, even when I had financial freedom in real estate, I kept jumping into other things that tied up my time. I was still grinding just as hard, even when I didn't need to.

Eventually I had to tell myself, *You don't need the money. You love to compete. You've got an amazing family. You love to give back. You can do the things you love. And you can say no. That's okay. Somebody wants you to come speak in Houston? You can say no. A new opportunity comes your way? You don't have to take it.*

Learning the power of saying no was just as important as learning how to work hard. Most people without capital fail early because they don't work hard enough when they have to. But another mistake is failing to ease off once you've earned the right to.

In the end, your goal is to enjoy this life. Enjoy your family. Enjoy your time. Buy back your hours so that when you want to do something with the people you love, you don't have to ask anyone for permission. You don't have to wonder if you'll have enough to pay your bills or live the life you want.

## STEP FIVE: FIGHT BACK AGAINST FEAR

How come most people don't pick money? Fear. They're afraid. Of course they are—being fearless is abnormal. And a lot of us grow up being told that anything risky is bad.

When the broke people around me gave me advice while I was growing up, I didn't listen. My mom, my uncle, my friends—all broke as shit—giving me advice on life. By the time I was 11 or 12, I was tuning them out completely. I couldn't tell you what they were saying. I had the magic ability to look them right in the eye and tune them out.

That's the power of knowing who you're around, who your source is, and what you're trying to accomplish.

They weren't bad people, but there wasn't any financial advice they gave me that I followed. I had disdain for their opinions because I didn't want their life.

When I talked about what other people had made or done, my mother would always nicely remind me that it's not as easy as you think. Maybe they were given that. And it always felt like she didn't believe I—or anyone else—could get the things other people had. We were broke, and in her mind, we were going to stay broke. I fought that thinking hard.

Adults don't like it when you don't give a fuck what they think. That caused me problems as a kid. But I was like, "Dude, you can hit me, you can ground me, you can take stuff away from me, but when I turn 18, well, y'all can do whatever you want, but you're not living the life I want to live."

It wasn't about being rich—it was about not being broke. I didn't want to hear from broke people.

Same thing with my teachers in middle school. I hated them all, not just because they were unsuccessful, but because they were giving me advice on life in spite of being unsuccessful. And I was smart enough to watch where they lived, what they drove, and to understand they had nothing they could teach me—or they'd be doing it.

So I didn't want to hear advice from my teachers. I wanted to know what a kid in my class named Tom was doing. His dad and mom lived in a different neighborhood. They went on vacation. They had a nice car.

He didn't have to worry about what he bought. He didn't have to sell cookies to raise money for a baseball trip. I wanted to know what he knew, not what my English teacher, Mr. Helbig, thought he knew. He didn't know anything I needed.

That became my default attitude, even when it maybe didn't make as much sense. I played a lot of sports in high school—I loved baseball. I loved football. I didn't like basketball, but I played it because my coach made me. In college, I played baseball again.

But if my coach wasn't financially successful, I didn't give a shit what he thought. Once I realized I wasn't good enough to go on to play pro baseball, and was going to make money some other way, then what did I care what my coaches thought if they weren't even financially successful? They didn't know anything I needed to know.

When I was a baseball player in high school, my mentor and role model—even though he didn't know it—was a guy named John Ellis, who coached me in a summer baseball league before I went to college.

He wasn't my role model because he played professional baseball. It was because he was financially successful.

I wasn't trying to play for the Rangers, Yankees, or Red Sox like him. I just wanted to have what he had. I wanted to build a successful life and take care of my future kids. I didn't want to worry about where I lived. I didn't want to wind up being some guy worrying about buying formula.

So I listened to him because he was successful as a businessman, and I wanted to know what he knew. That was my criteria for taking advice: You didn't have to be rich, but you couldn't be broke.

## STEP SIX: TAKE RISKS—JUST NOT THE STUPID ONES

You saw me take some risks in the first chapter. I'm not risk-averse. But I'm not taking stupid risks, and neither should you. Some things are just too risky. Say you're thinking of robbing a bank. The risks are pretty obvious, right? You could get shot. You could go to jail for a really long time. Even if you're okay with stealing, which you shouldn't be, it's just not worth the risk.

But a lot of people have the same attitude toward something like real estate investing, which many people seem to consider as risky as robbing a bank. You could put a couple of hundred grand into a piece of land you want to develop, but most people don't, because they have been conditioned to believe anything that has risk is dangerous. That's why such a small percentage of people in America hold such a large percentage of the wealth: They focus on the opportunity more than the risk.

Most people are afraid of everything. They're afraid of what others will think. They're afraid of pushing people away. They're afraid of being alone—because picking money can be lonely. Don't fear any of that. Believe in yourself. Why shouldn't you?

They also fear failing. And yes, when you pick money, you have to understand you will fail sometimes.

But here's the thing: If something doesn't go my way, I don't call it a failure. I call it a setback. And setbacks are part of the deal. The only real failure is quitting. So, as long as you don't quit picking money, you won't fail.

---

These six steps are the foundation of the picking money mindset. They're what I return to whenever fear, busyness, or excuses threaten to pull me back to old habits. If you stick with these steps, setbacks won't stop you. You'll keep moving forward. And as we move into the next chapter, we'll start looking at how this mindset shows up in real decisions—where money on the line reveals whether you've really made the shift.

But these steps don't change the reality that society itself is going to fight you every step of the way. The system is built in ways that keep people broke and dependent. In the next chapter, I'll show you how you can keep picking money even when the world is pushing against you.

→CHAPTER 2←

# REFLECTION QUESTIONS

1. Identify Your Impediment: Identify what's really holding you back. Busyness? Fear? Other people's opinions?

2. Find Your Mike: Who in your life will tell you the truth even when it's uncomfortable? If no one, where will you find that person?

3. Check Your Risk Filter: Write down one "risky" move that could accelerate your income. Now ask: Is it actually risky, or just uncomfortable?

CHAPTER 3

# PICK REALITY

## *WHY "DO WHAT YOU LOVE" KEEPS YOU POOR*

Growing up in Connecticut, we were poor, and I was raised around a lot of poor people. Behind our backs, the other kids in my school would call us "the apartment kids," because the neighborhood didn't have a lot of subsidized apartments.

And all those poor people around me always said, "Don't focus on money. Focus on your happiness."

The teachers I had never talked about me being monetarily successful. They talked about me getting a "good job." It felt to me like I was living in a culture that looked down on being poor but also didn't like talking about money. And I was right. That's our culture exactly. And that's what we're working against when we pick money. It's even harder on those who grew up like me, in families and communities struggling with poverty.

When I was 15, I was invited to play in a travel baseball tournament in Maine. I was on a team, but we didn't travel all over the country. My mom wouldn't have been able to afford that anyway.

The coach, who was a super nice guy, pulled me aside and said, "We'd love you to be on the team. I know I can't ask you because your mom can't afford it. But I will pay your way if you do me a favor."

I said, "That depends on what it is."

And he said, "I don't want your mom to know. I don't ever want her to feel bad."

And I thought, *Well, my mom's already going to know because I don't have the money. I'm working at McDonald's for $3.50 an hour. That's the* *money I use if I want a shirt, or a pair of shoes, or to hang out with my friends. It's not enough to pay for a trip to Maine.*

I didn't need people to pretend I wasn't poor. I needed people to say, "You're poor. Here are some ways to not be poor later in life."

But no one would tell me that.

My mom will say we weren't poor. But we lived in this tiny little apartment, and we didn't have any money growing up. People don't like being seen as poor. But if you don't have any money, what else are you? We lived in subsidized housing. My mom didn't go on vacation once in my entire childhood. She never just went out and bought something she wanted or spoiled herself.

I'm not saying any of this to criticize my mom. I'm actually bragging about her. I want to relabel her as a winner, a conqueror. She kicked ass in life. She raised her kids, and she kept us alive.

Seeing how hard she worked was what made me able to put myself through school.

But there's no getting around the fact that we were poor. And I'm driven every day by the way that society looked at me and my family. Sure, our society says, "Follow your passion." But if your passion doesn't make you rich, that same society is going to look down its nose at you.

## PASSION IS NOT A GOOD BET FOR YOUR FUTURE

People say if you do something you love, you'll never work a day in your life. It's something I heard in the culture I was raised in, and it's a common idea in American society. But it's also a lie, and the people who say it are lying to themselves. They'll tell you, "I could have what other people have, but I'd have to work more, and I'd have less time for my kids." Broke people are always pulling the parenting card—I don't have money, but I'm with my kids all the time.

I played baseball in college, and in my sophomore year my coach asked what I wanted to do after school. I said, "I want to play professional baseball."

He laughed and said, "There's no chance you'll play professional baseball."

When I asked him why, he told me, "You're six feet tall. This is how fast you run, how far you hit. You throw hard, but it's flat—it doesn't move. Tens of thousands of people can do what you do."

Then he said, "You're a really good athlete, but you're not a professional baseball player. If you do play a little bit, it won't be at a high level, and you won't make much money."

The next day, I decided to quit. I wasn't in a position to just have fun for the next four years. I needed to make money. So I got a job, switched majors, got my degree, and did an internship.

In high school, I thought, *I'm better than most of these dudes.* I'll *be at Yankee Stadium, playing third and pitching out of the bullpen.* Then I got to college and collided with reality. That dude was 6'4", 240 pounds. He hit the ball, and it left the state. I didn't hit the ball like that.

The coach who told me I wouldn't play pro ball was upset when I quit—he knew he'd win more games if I stayed—but he understood.

That wasn't all he told me that day. He also said, "You're very intelligent. You're a leader. People follow you. You're very gregarious"—I had to look that up later. "You're outgoing, and you can be very successful in life."

He said, "You could maybe play baseball for a few years and then be a coach, and that would be fine. But I think you can do great things in life." That breathed life into me. For that, I'm eternally grateful.

People say, do what you love. And for 0.1% of us, that's great advice. They're Kobe Bryant, they're Tiger Woods, they're Serena Williams. They do what they love, and they're wildly successful at it.

For the other 99.9%, doing what you love won't get you a secure life. It's choosing to struggle forever.

So when people say, "Do what you love," look at how they're doing. Ask them, "Is that enough for you?"

Because the reality is, there's nothing glorious about not being able to pay your bills.

And I mean that. There's no way in the world you can be in a good place when you're stressed about money, arguing about money, can't support your family, and don't have the money to help other people.

It doesn't matter if you have a job that feels like you don't work a day in your life—if you're broke, you're broke.

As a child, you're supposed to focus on your happiness. That's what makes childhood amazing. You don't have responsibilities beyond being a good kid. You don't have to worry about bills, going to work, or offending people.

But you're not a child now. So don't lie to yourself about what matters. You want to stop worrying about money. You want to pay your bills without even thinking about it. And once you create passive income and real financial success, you can do whatever you want, whenever you want. That's when your time really becomes yours.

It's not about your passion. It's about your strategy. Without a strategy, you could find yourself broke and stuck your entire life.

## POVERTY IS A TRAP

When I go into a Subway and see somebody in their eighties working behind the counter, I'm probably seeing someone who doesn't have a choice. If I were a betting man, which I am, I would assume people that age aren't choosing to work. They just have to work. They never learned how or had the permission to pick money. And now they're picking a job in their 80s. They're picking what they have to do to survive.

And a lot of folks are led down this path.

I'm not implying that person behind the counter is unhappy. Or that they've made a mistake. I don't know if they're happy or not with how their life has played out. But I'm betting that, at the end of the day, they never said, "I'm deciding to pick money for me and my family."

Our existence is very different depending on whether we're in charge of our money, or whether our lack of money is in charge of us.

One of the saddest things I see in America on a daily basis is people making difficult decisions about their health care and their medications based on what they can afford. Can I afford this? Should I risk spending on this? Can we do it?

People make decisions that are literally, brutally horrific for their health because they just don't have the money—a 2022 Gallup survey showed 40% of Americans putting off medical treatment because they couldn't afford it. The vast majority of people in America will admit they live paycheck to paycheck. If something pops up that exceeds their one paycheck in that period of time, they're in a lot of trouble.

People will say we have an awful system. But whether our system is awful or not, it's the system we've got, and we're not going to fix it tomorrow. So you have to put yourself in a place where you can counterbalance that system in your own life.

Picking money means making decisions based on what's best for you and your family, instead of based on what you can afford. With every company I launched, I put the training online for free. If other people used that information to compete with me, fine. We need to create a great, fair marketplace that actually lets people compete regardless of the resources at their disposal.

I wish a poor kid like me could have found information about business for free. I wish that when I was growing up, successful people had come to my school to talk to us about things like opening a company. I wish they'd shared that. Share what you've learned freely and openly, because everyone deserves the chance to do what you've done.

## EASY IS A MYTH

You can never be in control of your life or achieve financial freedom by coasting.

I used to smile inside when people would say, "It's going to be easy. I'll do this, this, and this, and I'll be rich."

I knew I'd have to work my ass off to get to a place where I could find or feel any freedom. The system isn't set up for financial freedom to be easy.

And there are people who feed that idea. Every day I see folks pretending to have a lifestyle they don't have. They try to sell people the bullshit that it's easy.

I can go on social media any given day and find people I personally know saying, "I woke up, I did this, I did that, I got rich."

I know their business model. I know for a fact they're not making anywhere close to the money they claim. And they're faking proof. Friends will say, "Hey, man, I saw a picture of your plane on Instagram," and when I look, it's a stranger who's pretending my plane is his plane to prove how successful he is.

People are weird, and I'm fine with that. I'm not judging. But what bothers me is when they use it to lure people into giving them money. "*Listen* to me and *you'll* have a plane just like mine." Except they don't own a fucking plane.

Take pictures of whatever you want. Say you make $142 million an hour—I don't care. But the second you start saying, "Come to me, give me your time, give me your money," *then* it's a major problem.

So when people tell you, "It's easy to make money. I got rich without breaking a sweat," they're lying.

Because here's the truth: Picking money is a grind. A motherfucking grind. Six or seven days a week. Twelve to sixteen hours a day. Lack of sleep. Sacrificing things you like to do—working out, hanging with friends, watching sports, whatever.

You lose time with your kids. I sacrificed that time for a short stretch so I could spend the rest of my life how I wanted—making my own choices, spending time with the people I wanted to. You can have that, too, if you build a business. But you can't avoid the grind. If you think you can, you're lying to yourself.

Skip the grind, and you'll never truly pick money.

## YOUR TOP THREE GOALS

Right after I picked money, I sat down and figured out my top three ambitions. You'll hear people say, "What is your why? What's your North Star? What guides you? What motivates you?" These were my whys . . .

Number one: I didn't want to live my life worried about money. I wanted to make enough so it would never be a concern.

Number two: I wanted to put my family in an income bracket nobody in my family had ever been in. I wanted to do something for my last name, my mother's maiden name—anybody related to us. I wanted people to stop looking at us like broke asses. I wanted people to stop feeling bad for us or thinking we were below them.

You're not a better person, or a worse person, for being broke or for being rich. But being poor makes people think of you as less than. And I wanted to change that perception.

Number three: I wanted to help other people live without worrying about money. I wanted to help them put their families in a different income bracket. I wanted to replicate and duplicate what I was doing so others could rise too.

You have to start by thinking about what you want to achieve and point your life toward that North Star.

When picking those goals, you need to be honest about what you want. Maybe your buddy's doing this, or your spouse or father is telling you to do that, and you're thinking, *I don't give a shit about money. I just want to hang out with my boys.* Chances are you're lying—we don't live in a society where you can truly not care about money—but that's okay. If you had asked me at 21 to pick money, I wouldn't have done it. I wasn't there yet.

You have to be honest with yourself so your life mirrors what you actually want. What you focus on is what will grow. That's just common sense.

So, being honest with yourself, pick your top three goals. Write them down. You need tangible goals to work toward, even if they change someday.

Mine haven't. I set them over 20 years ago, and they're still exactly the same. How? I keep them in front of me. Every week, I check in: Am I still working toward these? Do they still drive me? For 20 years, the answer's been yes. But if yours shift, that's fine. Just make sure you're checking. Goals that live in a drawer don't do shit for you.

## CHANGE YOUR MINDSET

Growing up, I watched my mother work harder than anyone I knew, never getting ahead, trapped in a system that kept her trapped, and a culture that told people like us to stay down where we belonged. I knew that wasn't the way to live. And when that coach told me I'd never play pro ball, I didn't throw up my hands in despair—because I knew there were still other paths, and nothing was going to stop me.

If you think you can be stopped, it's time to change your mindset. You can become an absolute savage in your work ethic—your grind. You can become an absolute savage in your mindset, where nothing rattles you.

And if your attitude, mindset, work ethic, and grind are all at that savage level—where 99% of people look at you and say, "*Damn*, that dude's different"—that's how you pick money.

That mindset has taken me to a place where I don't worry about money. I've lifted my family into a different income bracket.

And through my company, Family First Life, I've helped tens of thousands of people to do the same. I developed a sales system that the average person can understand, and my tens of thousands of independent contractors prove that anyone can be good at sales, even if they have no experience. Even if they've never sold anything. I could hire you today, whoever you are, and have you making four hundred grand next year, because it's easy. I can get anybody to do it.

Do I feel like I've never worked a day in my life? Absolutely not. It's been a lot of work. But that's what got me where I wanted to go.

But you can't just pick money and work your ass off anywhere. Working hard in the wrong place will keep you broke, just like working easy anywhere else. In the next chapter, we'll talk about how to pick where the money actually flows.

→CHAPTER 3←

# REFLECTION QUESTIONS

1. Follow the Money, Not the Dream: What industry pays well that you've been avoiding because it doesn't "excite" you?

2. Calculate the Cost: If you keep following your passion for the next five years, where will you be financially? Be brutally honest.

3. Spot the Conditioning: What messages about money did you grow up with? Write them down. Which ones are keeping you broke?

CHAPTER 4

# FIVE YEARS TO FINANCIAL FREEDOM

*THE PICK-MONEY PLAN*

We've talked about why you need to pick money, what mindset it takes, and why following your passions keeps you broke. Now it's time to build your plan. Five years is the right timeline—soon enough to be tangibly close, long enough to actually change your life. In this chapter, I'm going to show you how to set your income targets, build a budget that works, develop discipline, and hone the skills that make you valuable. By the end, you'll have a five-year plan you can start working today.

My plan, when I took my job at the State of Connecticut, was to grow my income by 100% over five years. And to do that, I needed to grow my income by 20% each year.

There was no way I could grow by 20% every year working for the state because a promotion did not result in a huge income increase, and there weren't enough levels for me to move up to in a year to make that annual 20%.

That's when I got my real estate license and took on additional work. I realized that if I couldn't achieve my growth goals through my primary job, I needed to find another path. When I discovered the right industry and position, I saw that I could leverage both simultaneously.

Why don't most people take this approach? Simple—it requires tremendous effort to manage a full-time job, a personal life, and an additional career. But I wasn't looking for just any part-time work that would keep me trapped in multiple capped-income positions for the rest of my life. I was picking money in a way that would ultimately give me control of my environment and my situation.

For me, real estate turned out to be my perfect industry, even though I had a pretty decent job at the state and was focused on moving up there.

But unlike a lot of people who are afraid to make changes, I was ruthless in making the changes I needed to make. I was willing to deprive myself of things I wanted and give up another 30 hours a week of my free time because my focus was on how I could control my environment instead of letting it control me, and how I could control my money instead of a lack of money controlling me. And to do that, I had to stick to my five-year plan.

I wasn't looking to quit my job overnight. I think that a lot of people start working and receiving extra income in a part-time job or as a consultant or something, and all they're thinking is—*Man, I can't wait to quit my job.* But all I was thinking was *I can't wait to be financially free.*

I kept my whys intact. I knew where I needed to be, and asked myself—"Is this going to allow me to achieve a higher income bracket than anyone else in my family has ever been able to pull off? Will it be something that allows me to change my life, and then go ahead and change other people's lives because of what I'm doing?" That future is what mattered.

Every decision I made was in line with my why. And any decision I made was made to allow me to get to a place where I was no longer worried about money. And knowing what I wanted my life to look like allowed me to combat any fear that popped up. Fears like:

- What if I don't make it in real estate? Well, who gives a shit? I need to get ahead.
- What if I regret doing this? Who gives a shit? None of that matters, because what do I have to lose?
- Will I lose time? Am I going to have fewer friends? Who gives a shit?

What fears are you currently wrestling with?

In this chapter, I'm going to walk you through six steps that will help you build and execute your five-year plan. These aren't theories—this is exactly what I did, and what I helped thousands of people to do to pick money and achieve financial freedom.

## STEP ONE: SET YOUR INCOME TARGET

Set your money goals by figuring out what you want your life to look like in the next five years. Do the math. Write it out. Keep figuring this out as you move up the ladder. Where do you want to live? What will your mortgage be? Be as specific as you can be.

When I turned 40, I told myself that I'd buy my first million-dollar-plus house. And I bought one for $1.2 million. Then I bought one for $3 million, then $5 million. But at the end of the day, I knew specifically what I wanted to do and when I wanted to get there.

I knew what I wanted to put away. I knew how much I wanted to earn on my money every month. I knew how much I wanted in tax-advantaged municipal bonds and how much was going to be in equities.

I knew where I wanted to go, and I was very detailed in my financial planning. So when I met with financial advisors—who changed as I continued to move up so I would always have the right person to manage my money—I was clear on what I wanted: to be financially secure for the rest of my life.

I believe your money goal should be to grow your income to where you have a liquid million dollars and then start scaling that exponentially. If you can get to a million dollars liquid, you continue to grow your income, and you look at the things you can do with your money, the success is astronomical. What's your required monthly savings to get there? You need to break it down by month, by quarter, and by year.

What does it look like after five years? Make sure you know exactly what your progress should be. Track it, like people track their intake of calories.

## STEP TWO: BUDGET

One key habit you need to develop is budgeting. When I set up a lifestyle that was affordable and supported growing my wealth, my bottom line was—don't spend money carelessly while trying to build my future independence.

Most people don't have any kind of budget at all. They don't have any awareness or discipline. Being financially free requires discipline. Even after you've built your wealth, stay sensible.

Create a pile of money. Create enough wealth where you can live off that pile of money. Decide what you need to live on—$10,000 a month, $20,000, $250,000—and allow your pile to earn that money for you through the market. Be sensible, diverse, and intelligent in your investments. Find somebody to help manage that for you.

But no matter how big the pile, no matter how much income you make off that pile, you still have a budget. You're going to be at a point in your life where you're buying everything you can imagine—private jets, yachts, expensive cars, and expensive houses. And I promise you, no matter how much you've got, unless you're one of the top four or five wealthiest people in the world, your money can still go as fast as you get it.

You might say, "Well, I want to make a million dollars a year." If you make a million dollars after taxes and you're spending $930K of that, then you're still broke. It's no different than if you make $80K after taxes and spend $60K.

I try to be sensible in my spending. It doesn't mean that I'm not buying a lot of stuff, but I'm being as sensible as possible.

I think about what I need to purchase. As soon as most folks have more money than they thought they'd ever have, they blow it. And that's the reason one of my whys is taking my family to a different level.

I still carefully maintain my budget. Why wouldn't I?

Most folks that have found a way to make money lack discipline. They can't keep it, utilize it, or grow it. But when you know your budget, when you create discipline, and you're picking money, you become really, really dangerous—in a good way.

My company had a budget. We knew where to spend our money. We knew what ROI we were getting. People would come in and say, "I thought the office would be bigger and nicer." I'd say, "We can lower your compensation, lower your pay, and get a bigger office." They'd say, "No, I think the office is great, Shawn."

## STEP THREE: BUILD DISCIPLINE

Budgeting is one of many things I'm asking you to do that requires discipline. And the magic to being disciplined, if there is any, is acknowledging the negative ramifications that will be created by your lack of discipline. What if you can't pay your bills? Can't support your family, can't provide for your kids, can't get good health insurance, can't get medications for your mom, can't raise your kids in a good neighborhood?

Discipline is achieved when you realize that the negative ramifications of not being disciplined far outweigh the pain, the discomfort, and the sacrifice that discipline takes.

Discipline just comes out of building the right habits.

So, when I worked at UPS, I got up at four every morning. But even though I worked five days a week, I didn't sleep in on the weekends because I wanted getting up at four to become my body's habit.

And when that alarm went off at 4 AM, and it was two degrees out, and the floor was cold on my bare feet, and it was so dark that it felt like the world was saying, "Bro, what are you doing? You should stay in bed," I never hit the snooze button. I was up. I was after it.

Mainly because I feared what would happen if I listened to that voice telling me to take it easy for a bit. I've always felt like I was competing with somebody out there working to take away my market share. Somebody who could do my job better, whether I was working at UPS or running my real estate company. That somebody wasn't hitting the snooze alarm, and I couldn't give them 10 minutes on me. That fear outweighed the coldness of the floor and the comfort of the bed.

I work out seven days a week. Why? Because I am afraid of what will happen to my health if I don't. Even though there are times when I don't want to do it, I always think about what happens if I start skipping days.

That's the same way I got sober. I still thought about drinking and getting high, but I kept thinking about the negative ramifications—flashing back to jumping off a balcony at a hotel onto a car and getting injured beyond belief and bleeding all over the place.

The power of habit goes both ways. When I create good habits, it gets easier. After you wake up at 4 AM for a while, it just becomes a habit. And if you hit the snooze button every day and don't get up, that becomes a habit.

Habits are hard to break. Why would I not want to have great habits that are hard to break?

If you want to be disciplined, then create an abundance of great habits.

## STEP FOUR: FULLY COMMIT TO PICKING MONEY

It really amazes me how many people are unbelievably disciplined in terms of their health. They'll go to the gym X hours a day and count macros. They are rabidly committed, but they're still broke. And if that's the case, you're rabidly committed to the wrong thing at this time in your life.

Ideally, you'd be committed to both—build up your body and build up your finances. But when you can't pay your bills, you can't be financially free, and you can't support your children but you're in the gym that many hours a day, you have the wrong priorities.

It's one thing if you're putting your hours into something that could lead to a profession. If you want to be a professional guitar player, and you're practicing guitar six to eight hours a day to be great, then cool, you're working your craft. How many years are you going to do that until you monetize it? Maybe you say, "I'll give it everything I got for two years, and if it doesn't work, then I'm just going to get myself a job and do your five-year pick-money plan. But right now, what I'm going to do is try to perfect my craft."

And I get that. But you aren't going to get paid because you can do X amount of curls or crunches. Nobody cares. So you just need to understand these things as you're moving forward. And as you continue to become disciplined in your budget, become disciplined with your money, and become disciplined in your approach, you have to start to hone your skills.

## STEP FIVE: LEVEL UP YOUR SKILLS

If you're serious about rapidly climbing the ladder in your job or in your business and making more money, skill development isn't optional. It's part of your financial strategy.

I mentor a young man named Tyler who is constantly learning new skills and always advancing. His business is restoration—plumbing, mold mitigation, emergency services.

Tyler is always developing additional skill sets. Every time he has an opportunity, he looks around and says, "What can I do next? What can I do to put myself in a better position? What certification can I get that will further my opportunity?"

You would think that would be the norm. I mean, why wouldn't people learn skills that would make them more valuable and let them make more money for their families?

And yet, when I worked at the State of Connecticut, where you had to have a master's degree to get promoted, a lot of people wouldn't do it, even though the state offered full tuition reimbursement. You finish these classes, you get the minimum grades, which I think was like a C and above, and they would fully reimburse your college costs.

When I went and got my master's degree, which took me a year and a half, I was blown away that people didn't do that. It said in the guidelines, in our book, you cannot be promoted to that supervisory position without a master's degree. And so they were just forgoing a promotion when all they had to do was get a free education.

But Tyler is continuing to learn new things. Still receiving additional certifications. Still asking, "How do I get licensed to do this? How do I get preferential treatment on this? How do I get to know more about this so I can take these additional classes and get these additional licenses and accreditations?"

And the reality is that a lot of his peers in the business won't do it. They know what they know and that's all they want to know. But Tyler has become a one-stop shop, basically. Whatever you do in that space, come to him. He does it.

A lot of people get their jobs when they're younger, and then they're older and they think, *I put in my time—you have to put in your time and pay your dues*. But I wasn't interested in just putting in time. I don't gotta pay my dues. What does that even mean? I am going to work my ass off, be more productive than anyone else, and bring more profitability to the company.

If I'm working as a social worker, I'm going to be better at protecting children and families. Don't tell me that what makes you more qualified is just being here checking a box, showing up every day with your lunch box. That's bullshit. That's not the winning dynamic.

So, every opportunity you're in, you should be thinking, *What's my game plan? What is my vision to move up?* Always look at whether you're taking advantage of what's there for you.

Not everybody thinks that way, but the people who do have an advantage over everyone else. So when I saw how Tyler was always educating himself, I knew he was going to win.

You may not have any idea what it is you need to do to move to the next level, which is why you need to ask. When you're having your annual evaluation, ask your manager, your boss, your supervisor—"What do I need to do to get promoted? What is holding me back?" And if they say, you need to know this, you need to be educated in this, then you go out and you find where you can learn what you need to know.

I had my epiphany to pick money in my late 20s. I was excited, I was focused, and I was glad I had decided to pick money for my family. But I wasn't sure I knew what I actually needed to do.

I figured out that I'd have to get connected with people who knew what I should be doing and become an unbelievable student.

Mentors, teachers, and coaches love good students. It makes them want to teach.

Recently I asked Tim Grover, "Since you worked so closely with Michael Jordan and Kobe Bryant, what was something that most people don't know about both of them?" And he said they were two of the best students he ever had. They never, ever, ever wanted to stop getting better. They were so committed to learning, and were always asking—"What do I need to change now?"

Now, most people in the world, if they achieved anywhere near their level of success, they would say, "Hey, I don't need to learn anymore. I don't need you, Tim Grover, pushing me to go further. I've got my stuff figured out."

But not Jordan or Bryant. No matter how successful they were, they kept saying, "I gotta get better. Tell me how to get better."

So find the people who can teach you what you need to know, and never stop learning.

## STEP SIX: UPGRADE YOUR TEAM

I haven't filed my own taxes in a long time. I have an accountant. But the accountant I have now isn't my first, or even second. I've changed accountants a number of times as I've progressed up the financial ladder.

When I started buying private planes, yachts, and real estate, my accountant at the time didn't understand anything about them. He didn't have that kind of experience. So I moved on to someone who had the skills and the knowledge I needed.

Most people are not going to tell you they're no longer the right person. People don't always recognize that they're out of their depth. They coach Little League and think they could coach a professional team. They work in accounts and think they could run the company.

So you have to make these decisions as an investment in yourself.

I see so many people who stay working with people who are allegedly helping them. But they're not being helped, they're not growing, and they don't want to say anything because it's uncomfortable and they don't know what to say to them. What do I say to them? What happens if they're mad at me? What happens?

But I was never afraid to say—hey, it's been great, but I've now outgrown what you can help me with. I wasn't worried about my accountant being mad at me when I told him I was moving on. Not once. With my attorneys, I've moved from a couple of hundred bucks an hour to $500 to $800 to $1,400 an hour. Because the scale of the things they deal with is bigger.

At the same time, don't add people to your team before you need them. Take financial planners. When you're young, you have nothing. If you go to a financial planner, they need to charge you for something, so they come up with a financial plan for you. They tell you what the cap on your rent should be, what your car payments should be.

But when you don't have much, a financial planner is like a personal trainer, mainly there to offer you motivation and make you feel someone will be let down if you don't do the right things.

If you're disciplined, you don't need a personal trainer telling you to do exercises you already know or a financial planner to tell you to stay in your budget. And if you're only doing it because someone is telling you to, eventually you'll just stop. But if you do it because you're thinking about how you'll let yourself and your family down if your spending goes out of control, that will keep you on track in a way a financial planner can't.

People argue with me on this—they say, it's hard for people to be disciplined and accountable. But if you need to hire somebody to tell you not to spend money, my take is that you lack commitment, are lazy, or don't have your priorities in order. If you go to the gym and need to hire a dude to count reps for you, you're acting like a dumbass. Be a fucking adult.

And be an adult who has a plan. Income target. Budget. Discipline. Full commitment. Uplevel your skills. Upgrade your team. That's what it takes.

This week—not next month, this week—write down your five-year income target and break it into what you need to make every year to get there. Set up your first quarterly check-in. Put it in your calendar right now.

Do this, and five years from now you won't be wondering when things will change. You'll be living the life you picked.

→CHAPTER 4←

# REFLECTION QUESTIONS

1. Run Your Numbers: What's your current annual income? Multiply it by 2.49. That's your five-year target using the 20% annual growth model. Write it down.

2. Identify Your Gap: Can you grow 20% per year in your current job? If not, what needs to change?

3. Map Your Income Growth: If you can't hit 20% growth in your current role, what's one way you could earn money outside of it starting this month?

CHAPTER 5

# PICK YOUR INDUSTRY

*FOLLOW THE MONEY*

Nobody wins in the wrong job or the wrong industry. It's one of the first tangible things we can fix. Do it now.

When I worked for the State of Connecticut, I had a green book that showed which level I was at as a social work supervisor—SH-26, if I'm remembering correctly. That level determined my income for every year, no matter how well I did my job. As we moved up, every one of us had a tiny increase in salary. Literally tiny. And when I decided to pick money, I realized that, at the end of the day, I was in the wrong job. I was making a living, but I was also stuck.

I want to be clear. Jobs aren't evil. The world is filled with so many fake, wannabe entrepreneurs and businesspeople who are always talking about how jobs are evil, how jobs suck. That's a lie. I've always had a job. I had a job when I was building my business. Jobs are a good thing. But you need the right one if you don't want the job to end up owning you and your time.

The wrong job for me was one where I couldn't increase my income. One where there was no upward mobility possible, where it was all seniority-based, and I couldn't move up unless I'd been there between 10 and 40 years.

When I think of people who were in the wrong job and then flourished when they got the right one, it often involves people leaving W-2 jobs to be 1099 independent contractors.

For example, I have a really, really good friend named Chris. When I first got to know him, we were both working for the State of Connecticut. He was in the wrong job too.

I was working as a supervisor, supervising social workers in the field. Chris was an investigative social worker who worked at what we called the care line—he didn't work in the office, but he was on call for a set amount of hours a week. So we could call Chris at three o'clock in the morning and say, "Chris, I need you to go to New Haven because we have an investigation." And Chris would get in his car, drive to New Haven, and do the investigation. And I would see him at the office when he came in to write his reports.

Chris came to me one day. He was complaining about the hours. Complaining about not being able to do stuff with his family. Complaining that if his daughter's birthday was on whatever day, he could never control when he was called. His family had to run their lives based on his work schedule, and he hated that. So I said, "All right, dude, I agree with you. That is a problem. What is your solution? You like the job, and it's what you have right now, but you don't like how it controls your life. So, what if you take a job working in here Monday through Friday, eight to four? Would that help?"

But he said, "No." There were issues with that as well.

This was my last year in social work. I was already also working in life insurance at that time, so I was winding things down with the state.

So I talked to Chris about becoming an independent contractor. I told him why I thought it made sense for him. I said if he really hated being owned by his job, he had a skill set that he could utilize to make more money for his family and have more freedom.

But he never did it. He didn't believe he was a 1099, independent-contractor kind of person. And I didn't push it, because to be really honest, I didn't think he would ever grab the bull by the horns and actually do it.

So I left the state, and Chris stayed. And then, eight years later, I got a call from him. He said, "Hey, man, I thought a lot about what you said."

And I was like, "From eight years ago?"

He was still working at the state, still doing investigative social work, still going out and dealing with abused and neglected children, and the parents, and the perpetrators, at all hours of the night.

"I'm going to try being an independent contractor part-time," he said. So he got his insurance license and kept working at the state while he worked part-time with me as a contractor. And then, maybe a year and a half later, he quit his job at the state, even though he'd been there for God knows how many years, to work as a contractor full-time.

Now, at the state, he was probably making $130 grand a year, and that was with working a lot of overtime. But as a contractor, he went to making more like half a million dollars a year while working significantly fewer hours.

So why did Chris finally make that move? Well, a lot of times when people want to make a change, they watch other people first and see how it goes for them. So I think when Chris saw me leave and never come back, and then saw that I was doing really well, it validated that model for him. He thought, *It worked for Shawn. Why wouldn't it work for me?*

The transition wasn't that easy. A lot of people don't realize that to get out of your job, if that's your goal, there will be a short period of time where you'll work harder than you ever did before. Where you have to be like Chris, working a full-time job plus a part-time job that you have to work extra hard at because you're growing a new business.

But once you make it through that period, things get easier. Now, Chris is still working hard, but he controls his schedule. If his daughter's birthday is on Saturday, he doesn't have to work on Saturday. If they have a game on Thursday, he doesn't have to work on Thursday. He's spending a lot more time with his family.

Chris was in the wrong job when I first knew him. But now he's in the right one.

## THE BENEFIT TRAP

The greatest trick that capitalist employers ever pulled off was giving us benefits. They have us all scared. We'll give you full medical benefits, but you should never leave your job because you'll lose all that.

And we buy into it—I can't leave. I've got good benefits. And that keeps us stuck.

Actually, what really keeps us stuck is what we are told throughout our lives—especially those of us who were raised broke and uneducated about the actual power of money. We were told to go to school and get a good job. Then, when we got our good job, we were told to *never lose it.*

Now, if you're happy in your job, and there's upward mobility where you're able to make more money every year, keep reading. If you need help navigating how to get more money out of your current employer, I'll be getting into that. I'll explain how to leverage your job to make more money.

But first, you have to understand whether you're in the wrong job. Not a job you don't love, but a job that doesn't provide the financial results you need it to. One that doesn't offer the opportunity to have that in the future.

If you're looking for advice on how to get a job where you have no work, no stress, no income, and no upward mobility—you've got the wrong book. I never looked for that. And I've never believed in that. Even when I wasn't where I wanted to be, even before I picked money, I always knew I needed to find a way to have a better life. I was trying increasingly profitable industries, or what I thought were profitable industries—moving from social work to insurance to real estate. I just didn't really get there until I picked money.

## EVERY JOB IS TEMPORARY

I used to work at UPS. UPS made me money, but it also made me miserable.

It was making me miserable because the people who worked there didn't work as hard as I did. And it was the first time in my life that I realized there were companies that were run based on seniority, not on how hard somebody worked or how productive they were. And I hated it.

When the new list came out for drivers, it was all seniority. I would look at a name and think, *I deliver probably twice the amount of packages they can deliver per hour. I'm more efficient on my route. I don't complain. I do everything I'm supposed to do. But so-and-so has been here longer than me.* But I didn't perseverate about that. I knew that job was temporary—just a means to an end.

I never took a job and thought, *This is my job forever.* And I think that's a struggle for a lot of people. They can't see their job like that. But the job sees you like that. A lot of times, the employee sees a job as more permanent than the employer does. The job sees you where, if you don't serve a purpose for that job, the job will separate itself from you.

You have to understand your relationship with a job. When I took my job at McDonald's, I didn't think I was going to retire at McDonald's. When I took my job at UPS, I didn't think I was going to retire at UPS. When I took my job at the State of Connecticut, I never thought I was going to retire at the State of Connecticut.

I was using my jobs like they were using me. And I had no problem with it.

Now, even when I hated my job, I still did my job. When you're in the wrong job, that doesn't mean you don't work hard and give everything you got. It doesn't mean you don't maximize your ability to make money. And it doesn't mean you quit.

People want that perfect job, but I was never in a job where I was like, I don't like A, B, C, so I'm quitting. When I decided to eventually quit, it was because I had a better opportunity.

## WHY IT'S IMPORTANT TO HAVE THE RIGHT JOB RIGHT NOW

Don't wait to find the right job. Because one year becomes five, five becomes ten, and ten becomes the rest of your life. Once you're in your job, even if you realize it's not going to provide what you want for you and your family, it's harder to make a change after you've been at it year after year. The more time goes by, the more we get comfortable and become complacent. And then we don't know how to make that move.

So it's really important to be able to make more money now. Don't be 60 years old thinking, *God, I missed out on a lot of things I could have done for me and my family and the people I care about because I stayed in the wrong job.*

When you start a job, it might be the right job for right now, but you may grow out of that job, or the job might change. You need to be aware of when the job that seemed like the right job no longer fits.

That's one reason you don't want to use a job to make a new network of friends. I was never so enamored with socializing at a job that it made me uncomfortable to switch. I see a lot of people stay in jobs because of their friends at work, which is sad.

So, while I met dudes that I liked at work, I never forgot that I only took my job to make money for my family. If I built relationships and friendships—cool, I was happy about that. But the guys I hung out with outside of work remained the people I hung out with. With all the jobs I've had, and all the businesses I've run, those are still the people that are my friends. And I'll never lose them by changing jobs.

## CHOOSING THE RIGHT INDUSTRY

When you're picking an industry, you need to figure out where there's opportunity. You want a job in an industry that undeniably creates wealth for the people in it. And there are plenty of those jobs out there. I've had many high-paying jobs.

I have a friend named Eric who was in the wrong industry for many years. For over 20 years, he was in the car business, working as an employee 70 to 80 hours a week.

He was probably one of the greatest car salesmen you'd ever meet in your life. But even though he got promoted to finance manager and then to general manager, he still never could make the amount of money he wanted to make for his family.

So I suggested he could go into independent sales.

He asked what I would go into if it were me, and I said, "I'd do life insurance because there's no limit. Everybody's going to die, and there are plenty of leads. You'll spend fewer hours in life insurance to make more money. You're such a good salesperson, but you're using the wrong vehicle to get where you want to go."

So he went into insurance. And while in his last year in the car business he probably made around $300,000, which was a normal year for him, in insurance he had multiple million-dollar years.

And then he sold the life insurance business he had built for millions of dollars more.

Eric had spent two decades in the wrong industry. He was a great salesperson who works really, really hard, and all he needed was just to move to an industry where there was no longer a limit to how much income his skills could generate.

Start thinking about whether the industry you're in is going to allow you to actually make more money. A lot of these jobs are in industries that supply needs, not wants—real estate, life insurance, waste management, oil, and gas. The market for wants can shift with the economy, so think about the things people will always have to pay for. There are dead-end industries and dead-end jobs. A dead-end job is one where you don't know if you can ever move up. They will employ you and pay you, and as long as you show up, you have a J-O-B, but there is no upward mobility, no ability to negotiate a bonus, or make an additional commission.

You are just there to check a box on a daily basis. You show up, do your job, and go home. You make X amount of dollars, and you're always going to make X amount of dollars.

If that's where you are, you need to change jobs. I've sat with plenty of people who talk about how change is so impossible: They would never make a change; they can't imagine ever making these changes. They're afraid of taking a chance on something better. But you have to make that change or you'll always be stuck.

Pick industries that are essential, stable, and scalable. You want an industry tied to basic human needs that won't disappear—finance, real estate, engineering, anything tech-related, the health industry, food and beverage. I'd be careful with entertainment. Great industry, but there's often a cap on upward mobility. Whatever industry you choose, making sure you can move up is crucial.

For example, I loved being a social worker. I loved helping people. But once I realized that I couldn't support my family the way I needed to as a social worker, I started thinking about other industries. Where would I be able to serve people, make money, and move up?

## FINDING A JOB THAT ALIGNS WITH YOUR GOALS AND STRENGTHS

When I picked money, I knew I needed to find an industry that was essential, profitable, and fit my strengths. That's what you need as well.

To help you figure out what that would be, first list out:

- → Five reasons you're not making the money you should be making right now.
- → Five things that you want to accomplish in your life.
- → Five things you do well—your strengths.
- → Five jobs you think you'd like other than the job you're doing now.

One reason I wasn't making enough money was that social work doesn't pay well. I was proud of the 14 years I'd spent helping abused and neglected kids, and I wanted to continue to do good, but my income was capped.

One of my strengths was an ability to have uncomfortable conversations—I was already doing that as a social worker. And one thing I wanted to accomplish in life was to continue to help people.

So I thought about sales. It's one of the highest paying occupations in America. And I wanted to work in industries that sell products people can't live without, like real estate or insurance.

I thought I'd be good in sales, as long as there were leads. I didn't want to do cold calls—I'm not a tech guy who can come up with a new platform for generating leads.

I was unbelievably excited when I found the life insurance business fit both my needs and my strengths. Insurance helps people—it's a way to protect kids and families in the case of death and disability. It was a job I could feel good about, making sure families were protected. And I saw there were leads.

Also, I knew there was literally no cap. There was upward mobility in life insurance. I knew I could make myself indispensable. And I knew once I got really good at sales, I could make myself really good at management.

You may not have given much thought to what your strengths are, but you do have them. Things like your intellectual capacity. Your ability to communicate with people, problem-solve, and stay cool under pressure. Your ability to work harder than other people, pick productivity over comfort, see things before they happen, and act proactively.

Figure out which of those strengths you have. What are you most effective at? What are your skills? What part of your job do you feel most comfortable navigating through? Think about what you could do well. Ask other people who you trust and respect what they see as your strengths.

Next, determine which of your talents align with a role that offers you upward mobility and makes you indispensable. For example, athletes and former athletes are competitive and team players. Those skills align with sales, so when I opened my life insurance company, I focused on recruiting athletes. Sometimes it took some persuading—a lot of people in W-2 jobs are terrified of sales jobs—but I was almost always right to hire them.

Once you have an idea of what industry you want to work in, start talking to others in that industry to figure out what type of job you think suits you.

But don't talk to people who don't know anything. Often when someone comes up with an idea on how to make more money, they make the mistake of asking for advice. They tell four idiots they know who don't make any money that they're going to try doing something independently, and their friends are like, "That's a dumb idea. I wouldn't do that. That's stupid." They get talked out of it without ever giving it a real shot.

So determine your goals and strengths, do your research, and don't take the advice of anyone who isn't where you want to go.

## BEWARE OF THE JOB YOU AREN'T CUT OUT FOR

You want a job that aligns with your strengths but be careful not to take a job where your weaknesses will get in the way.

I have a good friend who should never have left his job.

It was a good paying job. He was making maybe $400,000 a year even though he wasn't the hardest of workers and wasn't going in to work weekends or nights. But after 14 years, he wanted to go independent and do something else.

And I told him, "Listen, you have to understand, being independent is a grind. Right now, you've got a Monday-through-Friday, eight-to-four job with an hour for lunch, weekends off, two weeks' vacation, and you won't have any of that anymore. You have to be ready for that."

But he never could get his mind around working until 11 PM or working on Saturdays. Like, he just could not do it.

And then by the time he finally decided that he wanted to go back, that job was long gone and he was in debt.

You really have to know who you are. If you're someone who just won't put in the effort necessary to succeed as an independent contractor, stick with your W-2 job.

## NEVER BE UNEMPLOYED

When I talk about finding the right job, I'm not saying to quit your current wrong job and look. You should never be unemployed. You always want to have money coming in.

And I mean never. When I was at the police academy, the deputy chief of police sat me down at this little police department in southeastern Connecticut and said, "We think we're going to go in a different direction."

They let me go Friday afternoon at five.

Friday evening I was calling people. I called a buddy of mine who knew another dude who knew a guy that ran a landscaping company. He asked when I could start. I said, "Well, it's dark now. How about tomorrow morning?" So he said, "Come to Point O' Woods in Old Lyme, Connecticut. See you at 6 AM."

So they let me go Friday, and on Saturday, I was cutting lawns. The guy at Point O' Woods gave me a piece of paper with a list of all the properties, along with a truck, a couple of lawn mowers, a weed whacker, and some gas. Small lawns, cottages, summer, huge development. I started working at 6:15 AM, and I had everything done a little past 7:30 PM, just as it was getting dark.

When I saw the guy, he asked how much I had done that day. When I said, "All of it," he exclaimed, "That was the list for the week!" I'll never forget this guy in his 80s saying to me at 21, "With that work ethic, you're going to be unbelievably successful." I really appreciated that.

Now, weed whacking wasn't the right job long term, but the point is, don't stop working while you look for that right job. Any job is the right job compared to no job. I don't understand people who don't have a job. I'm 52, and since I was 14, I've never not had a job.

I work. It's what I do. It's what I've always done. If you do that, you're going to have the same result.

## DON'T MAKE EXCUSES—MAKE A CHANGE

Change is hard. That's why most people never do it. So if you're one of the rare people who is willing to change, you'll get ahead.

I never made excuses as to why I couldn't change my industry. After my pick money epiphany, there was nothing I wasn't willing to do. I demanded no particular level of comfort. There was no part of me that thought, *Well, I'm just not going to be able to do that.* I never made an excuse.

I left jobs that would have been deemed good jobs. When I left the State of Connecticut after 14 years, people around me said, "You're leaving a good job." In response, I said, "It's a good job for you, but it's not for me anymore. It worked when I was in my early twenties. It worked when I was trying to figure out what I wanted to do. But it doesn't work for me anymore."

I'd gotten promoted a couple of times, then that was it. I couldn't go any higher. There were only a couple of people above me, and I realized that those people were not hired based on qualifications or merit. They were hired based on the relationships they had with the people above them.

And those people didn't like confrontation. They didn't like uncomfortable conversations. They only promoted people who would tell them yes. I'm not wired that way. My strengths did not match up.

My strength of being appropriately confrontational when someone needed treatment for their family in social work—and later when somebody needed to get life insurance—was not aligned with moving up. I would have to put all that away and just say yes to everything top management said.

In social work, my biggest strength became my biggest weakness. And that's going to happen to some of you as well. When it does, it will inhibit your ability to grow and make more money.

So, you have to stop making excuses. Even though change can be hard, the pain of regret is far greater than the little bit of discomfort you'll feel when you make that change.

Don't choose to make excuses because it's so uncomfortable to change. Don't choose the pain of looking back with regret on your decision to spend decades of your life in a dead-end job.

Don't wait. Find your strengths, look for your industries, and find your next job. Do it now.

→CHAPTER 5←

# REFLECTION QUESTIONS

1. Day One Question: If you started at your company tomorrow, what would you ask about moving up? Have you asked that?

2. Retention Check: How long have people been at your company? If turnover is high, why are you still there?

3. Are You Indispensable: If you left tomorrow, what would break? List three specific things only you handle well. If you can't, you're replaceable.

CHAPTER 6

# PICK HIGH CEILINGS

*HIGH PERFORMERS DESERVE HIGH REWARDS*

Since my very first job at a supermarket when I was 14, I've been focused on getting ahead.

My mom was the hardest-working person I knew when I was growing up. She had a lot of jobs, and she always worked more than one job. She worked at a hospital up the street. Worked for a construction company. Did real estate for a bit. And on top of those full-time jobs, she'd do extra jobs like bartending.

She worked *hard*. If you paid her for 40 hours a week, she might work 60—*and* still do her part-time job(s). My mom's work ethic was impeccable. I remember once she was running in her clogs in the parking lot and she tripped and broke her ankle. So she put me and my brother in the car, drove us home with a broken ankle, dropped us off, and went to work.

My mother was a savage, even if it never resulted in the life she should have had—the life I was determined to get.

I felt an obligation to get a job so I didn't have to ask her for any money and I could help pay the bills. And at 14, in 1986, I was legally able to work and receive a paycheck, as long as she signed my working papers.

I went for a supermarket job because it was across the street from my school. I needed a job that I could walk to from school and then walk home from after. I wasn't old enough to drive, and I didn't want to put my mom out. Plus, even if she could give me a ride, there was no guarantee she'd have a running car. She had as many cars as she had jobs throughout my childhood—a VW Bug, a Buick Regal, a Toyota Tercel. All used, all unreliable.

I could walk to the supermarket from school in a few minutes, and then it was about a 45-minute walk home. So it was very doable, at least in the spring when I started working. I wasn't thinking ahead to winter, when I might wind up walking an hour home in a blizzard.

That was my first real job. My manager was named Buzz. And I remember thinking, *How did Buzz get to be in charge?* Anytime I saw someone running something, that was what I wanted to know: How did *they* get *there*?

I wanted to know how to move up the ladder. I was 14. Buzz was 80. I wanted to know the procedure to get from where I was to where Buzz was.

It wasn't that I actually wanted Buzz's job someday—God no. I did not see my future 80-year-old self being a grocery store manager. But I wanted to know how the process of moving up worked.

After our orientation, I said, "Where do I start?" And he told me, "Well, you'll start by bagging and getting grocery carts." And I was like, "All right, what's my next step up from there?"

I'll never forget what he said to me. He said, "Young man, if that's the attitude you have moving forward, you're going to do really well in life."

And I said, "Thank you, sir. I appreciate that. But still, what is the next job up?"

He said the next step up would be cashier, because then you don't have to run around the parking lot and bag the groceries. And then if you want to, you could try to move into one of the departments.

I asked if it would pay me more money, and he said it would. "If you become a cashier, you make more money. And if you go to any produce or deli department, or whatever, you make more money there. And from there, you can become a manager."

To which he added, "But you're fourteen." Which was a fair point.

I said, "Well, what should I be?" And he said, "If I were you, I'd become a cashier, and probably do that for a couple of years, and then probably go into one of the other departments when you're sixteen or older."

It wasn't a huge grocery store, and we had guys in those departments who had been working 20 years, so moving up wasn't ever going to be quick.

So I was bagging groceries and getting carts for a couple of months while thinking about how to become a cashier, then move into the produce or deli department to make more money. And then they decided to make me a cashier.

Weirdly enough, I didn't like it as much because it was easier work. I liked running around being busier. Being a cashier was kind of boring. But I did make more money.

After that, right from the start, any time I got a job, I started asking, "What's my next step? How do I get promoted? How can I make more money?"

I was at the supermarket for about eight months. Then, before winter came, I did what about one in eight Americans do at some point—I started working at McDonald's. And right away I asked them about what I could do to get promoted.

I was thinking more about this at 15 than a lot of people were at 20 or even 40. But it wasn't just that I was different from other kids. For me, that way of thinking was necessary if I wanted to help my mom and find a way out of being broke.

But here's the thing—you can start thinking this way, too, no matter where you are now. From the moment you start a job, you could be thinking: *What can I do to get more pay? To get a bonus? To get commissions?* You could ask, find out, and act on it. That's picking money.

## BE A HIGH PERFORMER

Early on, I learned the importance of working hard. If you want to move up, you need to be a high performer. And if you're not a high performer, then you need to become one. Being a high performer is free. All you have to do is work hard. That's all it takes. You don't have to do anything else.

Throughout my working life, there have always been other people around me who also wanted to move up. Again and again, I watched them not work hard at the job they had, then not understand why they didn't get the other job.

Once you commit to being a high performer, you want to work at a company where growth is actively encouraged.

I don't know that these conversations about how to get ahead at the grocery store or McDonald's would have taken place had I not asked, "How does moving up here work? How long will it take? What will that look like?"

I asked these questions at every job. When I got my job at the State of Connecticut, the first thing I asked after orientation was, "How long is it to get promoted?"

People looked at me like I was crazy. Like, why is he asking that? People who'd been there 30 years would literally come up to me and say, "I heard you're looking to get promoted." But I wasn't looking to get promoted right then—I'd been there for three days. I just wanted to know what the path was.

People said, "You need to put your time in like everybody else." But listen, I'm not like everybody else. Sorry. You shouldn't be either. Find out from the first day what it takes to keep moving up. Then do that full-out.

## UNDERSTAND WHAT YOU'RE IN FOR

Before you interview for a job, you should do your homework. Learn about the company culture. Go to sites that provide company reviews. Do a search on social media. Talk to people in the company who can give you insight into the culture. Ask them how long they've worked there. Do they have good retention?

I always look at a company's retention rates, whether they have 20 employees or 2,000. I want to know the average of how long people have been there. Because if nobody wants to stay, the culture is really bad, the compensation is really bad, or both. Or there's no upward mobility.

Make sure the company you're looking at is growing. How do you understand the company's true performance? Well, if it's publicly traded, then it's public information. You'll get more than enough if you look it up. If it's a small mom-and-pop shop or a one-man show, find out how long they've been in business. If it's half a year, be careful.

The company's past helps dictate its future, so you need to understand their journey. Find out what they were doing when they first started. What was their first year like? What were their goals and aspirations? You might be 22 years old and getting excited about a job, but you want to know what they did over the last 25 years, because this might be the next 20 years of your life.

Who's running the company? If it's a gentleman who's 84 years old, then what's their legacy plan? Who's next in line? Are they looking at acquisition at some point in time? If that happens, the most expendable employees will probably be let go. Because the way to make the bottom line look better is by cutting a lot of expenses.

How are they still in business today? Are they doing the same volume they did in year one? Or four times as much? What changes have they made? How many top performers do they have? What was their overall volume last year? What's their goal for next year? Are they looking to grow and scale or not? Because if you're looking to grow and scale your career, how are you going to do that when the company isn't?

## ASK QUESTIONS

In an interview, don't ever be afraid to ask respectful but pointed questions. I've always done that. I had a guy once say, "You have a lot of questions for a guy looking for a job." I told him, "I'm valuable. I can get a job at a lot of places. If the only job I can get is this one, you should be nervous to hire me."

I can remember interviewing at 21 with the State of Connecticut. I thought at the time that it would be an unbelievable job to have, but I still remember saying, "If you don't mind me asking, I have some questions."

"What's the company policy on raises and bonuses?"

"We don't get any bonuses."

"Okay, got it. What about raises?"

"Here's the way it works."

"Okay, got it. Is there anything that I can ever get if I go above and beyond?"

"Yes, you could end up getting overtime."

"Okay, got it."

People will say you need to be careful what you're asking in an interview. I don't know that I was ever that worried, but you can attempt to do it tactfully. I may not have been the most tactful applicant, but when I asked my questions, I was always honest, professional, direct, and very respectful.

Be clear in your interview that you're looking for a company where you can grow, because if they're looking to hire people who are not looking to grow—people who they think they can keep down, people who don't ever want to do something more than the average person—then if you're a high performer, that company's not for you. If they're not responsive, it's not a good fit for you because you're going to become frustrated. You're going to be mad at them.

But why are you mad at them? You're the one that made the choice. You joined a company that wasn't a good fit. If you want to grow your income and the company doesn't support that, then don't work at that company.

You're going to make a huge life decision that either allows you to grow your family's wealth or doesn't. So find a way to extract the information you need to make the best choice. You don't want to waste your time.

## DON'T BE EXPENDABLE—BE ESSENTIAL

At the end of my junior year of high school, my baseball coach made us all sign a contract. We had to agree that we wouldn't drink, wouldn't use drugs, wouldn't smoke, wouldn't break any laws, would have a good GPA, that sort of thing.

And that summer, before the school year started, me and a friend of mine got arrested—twice. Drinking, fighting, whatever. And I said to my friend, who was also on the team, "Dude, the coach is going to kick us off."

But my buddy said, "There's zero chance he's kicking us off the team."

I said, "No, look at the contract. It says if you break anything in this, you're dismissed from the team."

And he said, "Shawn, there's zero chance he's kicking either one of us off the team. We're too good. He wants to win games. He needs us."

But I didn't believe him. Because you wouldn't say you were going to kick someone off the team for breaking the law and then just not do it. That's not how things worked in my experience.

When my mom or dad said something, it happened. If they said, do that and I will beat the shit out of you, and I did it, they would beat the shit out of me. They didn't pretend. When I was growing up, there were no fake threats in my mom's apartment. There were no fake threats when I was spending time with my dad. None.

So we came into school, and the coach brought us into his office and started talking about our arrests. He was going on and on, going over the whole thing, and then finally he said, "I'll give you one more chance."

I'll never forget walking out of there. My buddy said, "I told you." He was one of those guys who wasn't really that smart but was a genius when it came to common sense.

And I remember thinking to myself, *That's wrong. That dude, our coach, he doesn't really care.*

I mean, it's not like we went out and committed armed robbery. But still, the rules were different for us because the coach would have less success without us. If it was two other guys who didn't play as well as we did, they would have been kicked off the team.

Now there are other coaches that would have had the courage to throw us off the team. But that coach, he really wanted to win. And me and my buddy gave him a much better chance.

As I look back on it, I think that if he cared more about me, he would have held me accountable. He'd have been like, "You're out, dude." I would have been devastated and upset, and he would have lost more games. But it would have taught me a better lesson.

Instead, it taught me that people will use me for what they can get out of me. But since then, I've used that to my advantage, because if they want to use me, then I know I've got leverage.

That's when I realized that if you're really good and really valuable, it's hard to mess with you. I thought, *I'm never going to not be good at something.*

You want to be essential in your role, not expendable. If you're working at any company and there's an economic crunch and you've been there for five years without moving up, they will cut the most expendable jobs. If you never bother trying to get promoted, you'll wind up being in one of those expendable roles.

When I worked for the State of Connecticut, they went through a phase of layoffs, and they laid off a lot of the people who were in entry-level positions. I had moved up a few times. I didn't want to be expendable, and they knew that I wasn't.

You're indispensable if you contribute effectively to the company's success. If I'm your supervisor and you do well, I do well—only a really weak supervisor would want to manage and supervise ineffective people.

People who are truly indispensable get treated differently than everyone else. When I took my first independent contractor position in real estate, there was a lady in the office who was a bully, had the nicest office, and never came to any of our frequent sales meetings.

I said to the manager, Gail, "Why doesn't she ever come to the meetings?" And she said, "She doesn't think she has anything to learn."

And when I replied that everybody's got something to learn, she said, "Shawn, she's just the number one salesperson. She's been that way forever. And there are just different rules for different people."

And that's the position you want to be in.

## KNOW THE METRICS

Make sure you're clear on what metrics the company is measuring you by. At UPS, for unloading trucks or for driving, the metric was packages delivered per hour.

When I worked at McDonald's, it was about food waste. We didn't want to throw food away, but it can only sit so long in the bin. So all positions had to plan for how quickly we could make whatever it was—including our average time per customer—regardless of whether you were a cashier or in the drive-through.

At the grocery store, it was how quickly you stocked shelves, or how many items you moved in a minute.

Every single industry has their own metrics to measure your performance.

Discover them. Then beat them. Every day.

## ADVOCATE FOR YOURSELF

Always be vocal. So many people are willing to accept anything because they're unwilling to open their mouth and advocate for themselves. So speak up.

At the same time, don't be one of those people who starts to advocate for themselves before they've done anything. They'll say, "I need to make my money," and the supervisor will say, "Well, you're not making us any money right now." That can cripple you, because if you start asking before you earn money for the company, everybody looks at you differently.

## OVERACHIEVE

Once you've got a job with that company you want to work for, you need to be a no-bullshit worker. You need to be a self-starter. At UPS, I took on extra responsibilities, and they put me in the preload, where I unloaded my truck faster than everybody else.

I gave them everything I had when I was there. I was excited because that was my job. They paid me to be there.

And people would say, although never to my face, "That guy's an overachiever." So, what are you saying? Does that mean I'm not lazy?

Hey, the more I unload the trucks, the better shape I'm in. It's healthy and I get paid for it. I wanted to make a good impression, have a productive preload, and get the drivers out on time to make their deliveries.

I wasn't afraid to take on other responsibilities. I would always say—tell me what you need me to do, and I'll do it. And I won't let anything get in my way.

When I was unloading trucks for UPS, even if it was cold and the rollers didn't work, I would unload my packages faster than anyone. And there'd be these guys unloading bags of mail, and they'd be going slow, so that even though they should have been done first and come back to help me, instead I would get to where they were and have them in my way. So I encouraged them to speed up by "accidentally" sliding the packages off the rollers and onto those bag guys, knocking them over. That was my way of saying, move your ass; you're in my way. And we usually came to some kind of understanding.

I didn't need to be in a supervisory role to want to work hard. I never thought my lot in life was to go to work, be friends with everybody, do as little as they did, and then die one day wishing I had done something more courageous—like continuously developing new and in-demand skills and getting certifications to stay updated and enhance my market value.

When I worked for the State of Connecticut, they said that if you got a master's degree, you could get promoted. I got a master's degree. When I worked at UPS, they said you needed certifications to get promoted. I got certified. Every job I've had, I did all I could to expand my horizons and make more money for me and my family—even before I had a family.

Once you know the path, stay laser-focused on it. The State of Connecticut said I needed one year before I could apply to be a supervisor.

The day I hit my one-year anniversary, I applied to be promoted. In every job, I kept track of that time frame.

If you don't understand your path to promotion or your path to making more money, then you haven't asked. If you've asked, and they haven't told you, if you're a high performer, then you're probably in the wrong place.

Now, if you're looking to just hang out and do your job forever, and you don't care if you move up or make more money, then it doesn't matter if you understand that path forward. But don't pretend that you want to be on that path. Just be nice and get out of the way when somebody else is coming through who wants to take that path.

## YOU DON'T NEED WORK FRIENDS

I've been to places where a lot of the people who worked there hung out with each other, went to happy hours, all this bullshit. Which is fine, except I was never there to make friends. There were some people I liked, some people I didn't, some people who liked me, and probably a lot who didn't. But I already had friends when I got my job.

When people only have friends at work, I always want to know, "Did you have friends before you worked here?" I see people get married, and everybody in their wedding party is someone they've known for eight months through work. What did you do the first 30 years of your life? Where were you? Do you not have any friends?

You don't take a job to make new friends. Somebody is going to get promoted. Somebody is going to make more money. It might as well be you. As a matter of fact, it needs to be you.

## EYES ON THE PRIZE

If you don't focus on the right things, and, you're not committed to your own success, why would your company care about you? Always ask yourself how you are viewed in your current job. Do they see you as being upwardly mobile? As being somebody who is important and valuable to the company? Somebody who should be making more money or have more responsibility? Or do they see you as one of the people much more focused on their work friends and getting along with everybody there, meaning, someone who's not a high performer?

Be accountable to yourself. Be accountable to the plan. Be accountable to getting promoted to make more money. If the company you work for doesn't have an upwardly mobile plan for you, and you're a high performer, get out now and find a different company. By now, you know a lot about what you need to do. Be indispensable. Ask questions. Make yourself valuable. Pick the right company. A place where you can grow, perform, and earn. Knowing what to do and actually doing it aren't the same thing. You can find your way into that perfect job and understand every strategy in this book, but if you don't have the habits and discipline to execute on them every single day, none of it matters. So let's talk about that.

→CHAPTER 6←

# REFLECTION QUESTIONS

1. Set Your Target: Where do you want to live in five years? What will your mortgage be? Get specific and do the math.

2. Build Your Budget: Track every dollar for one month. Identify three expenses you can cut or reduce.

3. Upgrade Your Team: List who helps you with money decisions (accountant, mentor, financial advisor). Are they where you want to be, or behind where you are now?

CHAPTER 7

# PICK DISCIPLINE

## *HOW HABITS CREATE SUCCESS*

John Ellis, who I mentioned back in chapter 2, was the first multimillionaire I'd ever met. When I realized how wealthy his business had made him, I assumed he was really, really talented. He was the wealthiest man I knew. I was just sure he'd been born with this amazing business talent. I assumed that he was probably a genius—that whatever he touched turned to gold.

I really wanted to work for him and see that magic up close, so I asked John for a job. I said, "I've already got a job, but I'll leave. You can give me a full-time job, or else I'll work with you during the day and I'll work where I'm working at night. Whatever you need me to do."

John gave me a job. After I'd been at it for about three weeks, I asked the workers about Mr. Ellis—how did he become so successful? And John's foreman, who had worked with him for years, said, "John is a guy that has conviction. He's a hard worker. He expects a lot out of us and out of himself. You're looking to think he's just unbelievably talented, but it's that conviction and hard work that have made him successful."

And when I started talking to John more, well, it's not that I wasn't impressed, but I just thought it was going to be supernatural. I thought it would feel like talking to the most brilliant, talented man I'd ever met in my life. It wasn't like that at all.

Since then, I've seen this over and over any time I've met people who'd reached a level of success that I wanted to reach. They were smart. They were steady, consistent, hardworking. But they weren't savants.

When I got into the waste management business, I went to meet with one of the national company's C-level executives. And I just assumed I was going to be blown away by this guy's ability and by the way he would process and articulate information.

But no. What I saw was that the guy seemed to have a really killer attitude. He was working his ass off. And he was good at building relationships, good at communication. But those weren't special talents, just skills he developed. He was a guy who had gone to high school and then started working at a waste management company and he'd just worked hard until he was making a lot of money in a very prestigious job.

So, the more I got around wealthy people and successful people, including the presidents of Fortune 100 companies, the more I saw that the common denominator was not their talent. They didn't need any talent—what their roles really required was perseverance, hard work, a great attitude, hiring the right people, and delegating to the right people. Successful people are great delegators of things they don't do well.

When I saw that, it blew me away. Because I could see that anybody could go ahead and do those things.

So, if someone lacks success, it's not due to a lack of talent. It doesn't require any talent to become wealthy and successful. Anybody who tells you otherwise is lying.

Earlier, we started thinking about a five-year pick-money plan. This chapter is the engine that runs it. My mind was blown when I learned that people like John Ellis aren't successful because of genius. They're successful because of consistency, dedication, stuff that's often pretty boring but crazy effective. Likewise, plans don't fail because the math is wrong; they fail because the habits aren't built. What follows is a series of simple, duplicable behaviors that can keep your plan moving forward and on track.

## LACK OF "TALENT" IS NO EXCUSE

At every job I was in, I said I would achieve more than everybody else. Was that because of my talent? Absolutely not, because none of them required talent. It didn't require talent to unload a truck. It didn't require talent to stock shelves. It didn't require talent to visit clients. None of those jobs required talent.

Whatever you might want to tell yourself, your job probably doesn't require talent either.

What it requires is developing the habits of discipline, willpower, and consistency. When we blame a lack of talent for our lack of success, we're just looking for a scapegoat so we don't have to blame ourselves.

Take this guy named Dominique. He was a kid when I met him—I think he'd just turned 20. I recruited him into the life insurance business. He was doing okay—selling some life insurance, making a few bucks—but I was pushing him to build an agency.

And he's like, "Dude, leave me alone. I'm not bothering anybody. I'm making eighty grand a year. I can't even believe I'm making eighty grand a year. I'm twenty years old, and I'm doing better than all my friends. So just leave me alone."

I asked him why he was so hard on himself, and he said, "You don't understand who I am."

And I said, "No, *you* don't understand who you are. Take this guy that does, like, X amount of volume a month and makes $4 million a year. What makes him different from you? Walk me through what makes him different."

What he needed to understand was that it doesn't matter what education you have had, or where you've come from. It doesn't matter if you're the smartest guy in the room. It doesn't matter if anybody had ever taught you anything about business.

If you are willing to be teachable, to work really hard, to have a great attitude, and to always develop yourself every day, then you can do anything that other guys have done.

It doesn't mean you're going to be number one. Everybody can't be number one. There's going to be a number one, a number two, a number eight, a number twenty—but you could be number 2,142 and still do really, really, really well.

So I told all that to Dominique. And I said, "You're scared because I believe in you. And I'm scared because you don't believe in you. You're scared because, if I'm believing in you, all of a sudden you might let me down. But you aren't going to let me down—as long as you work hard, dude, I'm good either way. I just don't want you to leave this much on the field or in the tank, bro. So you've got to get to work."

So, when people say, "I wasn't born with the talent—nobody handed me talent, and that's why I'm not successful," well, that's not it. They're not successful because they're fucking lazy. Or because they're undisciplined and don't have any willpower.

And all those habits are within your control. So, if you are lacking discipline, willpower, and consistency, that's 100% your fault.

The reason I get up every morning and work out seven days a week is that I want to be in a good place physically and mentally to be successful. When you have discipline, willpower, and consistency, you have what it takes to create your value.

I want to create value. The better I feel, the more value I will create in whatever I'm doing for anybody.

## WRITE YOUR HABITS ON A CLEAN SLATE

You need to have great habits. And where a lot of people fail when creating those new habits is they don't break their bad habits. They just add new habits on top. So you've still got all the shitty habits that are holding you back.

When I help people to develop habits, it has to be a clean slate. Here are all the things you should be doing to achieve success. Anything outside of that doesn't belong.

Wiping your habit slate can be challenging, as Dominique found out. Before I had recruited him into life insurance, he had been a talented athlete who played Division I baseball. He was a potential draft pick, although, ultimately, he didn't get drafted.

While he was working full-time with me, I was trying to get Dominique to use the habits he had developed when he played ball that made him successful. He had a commitment to getting better, and an undying desire to be the best athlete he could be. He was very coachable and willing to defer to people who knew more than he did. And he loved his teammates and always wanted to win as a team. Which is a great attitude in business—if you love to see your business peers win the same way you love to see your teammates win, you can build one hell of a team and people will follow you.

But while I wanted him to build on his good habits, I needed him to also get rid of the habits that had ultimately made him less successful than he could have been when he was playing ball.

A common problem with people who have been successful in sports is they have the experience of being able to cut corners and still be successful in the lower levels.

When I was an athlete in high school, I could do things well without practicing that hard. But I couldn't go to the University of Alabama and put in that same level of effort. I wouldn't have been successful and I sure as hell wouldn't get drafted because I didn't have that superior talent where I was so good that I could play at a professional level and still not work that hard.

But when you're young, and you're better at something than most of the people you're around, even when you're not putting full effort into it, you don't ever think, *I'm going to have to stop coasting someday.*

I would argue that if Dominique had combined his athletic ability with enough effort, he could have achieved a lot more. With enough commitment, he could have been an elite Division I player or a draft pick. He could, in my opinion, have been a professional baseball player.

But instead of focusing all his energy on becoming a top-class athlete, he hung out with a lot of people he didn't need to hang out with, engaged in activities that didn't help him in life, and was just focused on the wrong things.

So, when we started in business, he had the same old bad habits that had kept him out of the major leagues. And I was determined to get him to understand that athletic ability and talent are not a shortcut to success in business—his bad habits were going to eat him alive.

Dominique wanted to listen to me, but it was a struggle. He was trying to listen and to understand, but then he would just default to what he knew—hanging out with buddies, doing stupid shit, sleeping too late, and going out partying with no regard for anything. And when things got tough, he just shut down, ignoring things and hoping they would just get better.

Now, when he was focused on getting up early and not partying with his idiot friends, then he was having insane success. But he just couldn't put it all together because he was always fighting himself on that.

But when he met the woman who was to become his wife and they decided to build a family, it all changed. Because the best motivation to change is when there's something you don't want to lose.

It's no different than how I stayed sober because my daughter was on the way. Had I not had kids, the odds that I'd be sober are not very good. But I wanted a good relationship with my children. I didn't want to cause problems for them. I didn't want them to see me under the influence, making an idiot of myself.

So Dominique finally realized if he continued his bad habits, there was no chance for him to have the success he wanted for his family and for himself. His finances would always struggle. His family would struggle. His spiritual relationship would struggle. Everything would be a struggle if he didn't change these things.

It took that fear of loss to shake those old habits. But when he did, he never went back. And once he changed those habits, he was on the way to becoming a millionaire.

Once Dominique understood that it wasn't about talent, but ditching his bad habits and focusing on the strong positive habits that all successful people have, he was on his way.

Prior to that change, the odds were terrible that he would be a millionaire. But three years later, he was making a million dollars a year. And after that, he sold his company for millions and millions and millions of dollars.

To this day, 14 years later, Dominique still works with me. And he has a ridiculously successful financial life and family life, even though back then he was a young man with a T-shirt, sweatpants, and fear in his eyes saying, "Dude, just leave me alone."

## THE GOOD AND BAD HABITS THAT DETERMINE YOUR SUCCESS OR FAILURE

When I got into real estate, we became really successful as an agency because I created specific habits for all of us. Here are the days that we're going to make sales. Here are the days that we're going to work on marketing the current listings.

You need to create good habits where every ounce of time you spend on your business leads to profitability. But you can't create those good habits when you have bad habits already in place.

In real estate, bad habits include answering the phone and catering to everybody's requests for everything. Remember Craig, who I let run me all over town for weeks? Guys like him, who say, "I want to see 27 houses," aren't worth your time. That doesn't make you any money. Neither does the boss who says, "Hey, can you run around and put more signs up on the properties?" No, because you're listing at a price where it's not going to work anyway.

I created habits to minimize wasted time. We talk about waste all the time, like food waste. A restaurant doesn't offer 814 different dishes to pick from. They'd buy a lot of ingredients that would go bad before they could use them. But while everybody worries about things like product waste, time waste is just as important. That's usually the commodity in small businesses—your time. That's what you have to leverage.

When I got into life insurance, I asked, "How much do we need to sell a week to be profitable?" They told me what they thought, and I ran the numbers and realized—no, that won't make you profitable. You're not making money if you're selling less than this much a month.

So I created habits. I came up with the days we're going to dial, how many hours we're going to dial in a day, and how many leads we need to fill those hours. Everything was broken down into habits. And when you do it that way, it becomes very, very efficient.

The key was condensing time frames by eliminating conversations with people who didn't want our product. I only focused on speaking with qualified leads. For every sales company I looked at—whether door-to-door or cold calling—I said, "You need leads. Without leads, I can't help you. I can condense your time frames, but everybody that works for you is going to quit and go to lead-based sales." Because they should.

You can't create discipline without becoming a clean slate. So, in every business I went into, I wanted to look at: How are people making money? How are they losing money?

What habits can I pick that are duplicable? Getting up early is duplicable. Calling leads is duplicable. Buying leads is duplicable.

But if you say you must be able to pitch people for 45 minutes in a particular way, and you need to be on Zoom, and you need to share your screen, that may not be duplicable. There are too many moving parts for simple duplication. So I simplified the entire process, making it completely duplicable.

## DON'T MAKE YOURSELF LOOK BAD

Most people are struggling today because they don't want anybody to tell them what to do, ever. That attitude is encouraged by others. When people try to get ahead, they'll have friends and family and other broke-minded people saying, "You don't need to do that. Don't kiss ass—why are you trying to overachieve? You're making the rest of us look bad."

I used to say to my coworkers all the time, "I'm not making you look bad. You lazy fucks make yourself look bad without me. You look bad when you get up in the morning. You look bad all day long through the entire day. You don't even need my help to look bad."

Every job I ever had, I had a boss. And if he or she wanted me to do something that was part of my job, I did it. It didn't matter if I liked it. It didn't matter if I understood it.

I did it because my job was a means to an end, a way for me to become successful, a way for me to pick money, and a stepping stone for me to get to where I wanted to get to.

## KNOW WHAT YOUR BOSS WANTS AND DELIVER IT

It's important to know the priorities of whoever's above you—a boss, manager, supervisor, whatever they are. That's why you should schedule check-ins every three months. Your boss might only be scheduling an annual review, but that's not going to cut it.

Schedule something every three months where you sit them down and ask: What does success look like for me in the next three to six months? What five things that I do are most important for you? What matters the most to you? What do you need from me to make your job easier? And, most importantly: If I meet and exceed these priorities of yours, will I be on track for a raise and/or a promotion?

If they say yes, then boom, you've got an articulable goal.

Talk to your manager or boss about what you can do to make the company better. You can always bring them back to revenue. Are the things I'm doing helping you drive revenue? Was that one of the five things you said was most important to you?

Be confident, but not cocky. Cocky is running your mouth about things you can't do. Cocky is trying to convince yourself you're better than you are. Just be confident.

I'd always be confident, saying, "Here's what I can do for your company. Here's what I can do for you. Here's why I'm the best man for the job. Here's why I know that I am."

Based on what you've extracted from your boss, set your own goals. You need to set your bar and then blow past it. Set your deadline for each goal. Track your work. Look at how you impact things like efficiency, client satisfaction, team morale, and revenue.

## SOLVE PROBLEMS

Instead of being somebody who bitches and moans about problems, be a problem-solver.

Some people complain about problems that can't be controlled. They'll say, "Man, I wish we didn't have to get up so early to unload packages from trucks." But the guys who deliver them have to be on the road at eight, so you need to be there at 3 AM. That can't be changed. I always tell people, "Don't complain about shit you can't control." If you don't want to go to work so early, get another job. Some jobs are 3 AM jobs.

But there are some problems you can find and fix. You want to find gaps and solve problems before your boss even realizes they exist. Then tell them you did it, and how you did it. If you tell them you found and solved a problem, they can use that solution in another unit, another group, another department. So they need to know.

## THE YELLOW BELT PROBLEM

For example, at UPS, the yellow belt kept going down. Our conveyor belts were color-coded, and yellow belts were for the preload. When you unloaded the trucks, that was the first one it hit. Then it went to the splitter at the top of the belt who would be splitting the packages.

What was happening was the yellow belt would get jammed up. The preload would do their job and dump out so many packages, the sorters would throw them all in, but the guy or girl at the top couldn't split fast enough.

After having maintenance come out to look into it, I realized it was actually a work thing. The splitter needed to be doing a better job. So I walked up and said, "Hey, bro, get out of the way. I'm going to show you how to do it. You're going to watch, and you're going to learn how to do it. Because if I have to keep doing it, I don't need to pay you."

Sometimes that worked, but some people just wouldn't work hard enough. So I had to move them off the yellow belt to a different spot. I couldn't get rid of them because, with a union job, you can't get rid of someone for not doing their job well, which is mind-boggling. But by finding new places for the shirkers, I was able to keep the yellow belt running.

Now, when I solved the problem, I didn't want a gold star. I just wanted to continue to show how valuable I was—how not expendable I was. And I also wanted to find a way to make more money and get promoted.

So be proactive every day, all day, about your career. Record your data. Document everything. I could say when I went through my review—on this day, I was able to do this. I started here. This is how much I was doing. Here's how much I'm doing now.

Catalog your wins, your growth, your accomplishments, your losses, and leverage. Make everything visible.

## STAY FOCUSED AND UNCIVILIZED

The biggest struggle people have is they lose their focus. You experience a little bit of failure, and you bitch, moan, complain, and have a pity party. You say, "I'm just not going to work." You have a little bit of success, and you say, "Damn, look what I've done. That was so good, I deserve to take a week or two off."

Whether you fail or succeed, stay disciplined and locked in.

Also, stay uncivilized. Civilized demeanor is saying and thinking and doing things the way you believe you're supposed to. You need to take everything that would make somebody civilized and do the opposite.

It's uncivilized to go months and years sleeping two to three hours a week. It's uncivilized to confront people without worrying about their reaction. It's uncivilized to expect people to do better instead of just trying to be their friend. It's uncivilized to tell people the truth when it's really hard for them to receive. It's uncivilized to start talking about how much money you'll make in a year or five for a business you've just started that hasn't made a dime. It's uncivilized to tell someone, you've never made any money, but you can be making a million dollars a year in two years.

People who achieve greatness have an uncivilized demeanor. They work harder, sleep less, are more focused, and have a stronger mental attitude than most people.

I want to surround myself with uncivilized people.

## KEEP YOUR WHYS TOP OF MIND

Your plan doesn't work because you're talented—it works because you have the right habits. Get rid of the bad ones, build the few that actually make you money, and do them whether you feel like it or not. Stay uncivilized about your standards, treat your people right, and track your numbers obsessively. Do this consistently, and five years won't be some dream anymore—it'll be your reality.

Set up a system to keep reminding yourself of your three whys. Maybe every Monday morning, when you wake up and your week starts, you go over what is guiding you.

My why was—I want to live without worrying about money. I want to change the trajectory of my family and move up into a different economic situation. I want to help other people achieve financial success, just like I know I'm going to.

Then, at the end of every week, I gave myself an audit, reviewing and working on the things that actually mattered.

It can be dangerous to lose your momentum. It's easy for people to fall off track every once in a while. You have to choose not to. We've all had bad days or bad weeks. But you stay on track. If you fall off too much, it's impossible to meet your goals. Fall off too much and you start getting into self-deprecating bullshit—why you can't do it, why this bad thing makes it impossible, why you wish things were better.

But just remember, you're in a business that requires no talent. That means that success goes to the ones who work hard and stay on track. So when you fall off track, you need to adjust and get back on track immediately.

The habits of discipline, willpower, and consistency are not optional. They're the foundations you must have to move forward. If you don't understand the power of these habits, and cultivate them, then you'll be wasting your time. Nothing else will matter; everything will fall apart. And once everything falls apart, it's a wrap.

You're not going to get success based on whether you have talent—this is not a professional sporting event. You're going to get there because you have the right habits, or you're going to fail to get there because you refuse to be disciplined, to exert willpower, and to be consistent in those healthy habits. It's up to you.

→CHAPTER 7←

# REFLECTION QUESTIONS

1. Wipe the Slate: List your current habits. Cross out everything that doesn't directly support picking money.

2. Give It 90 Days: Pick a strategy and commit to 90 days before changing anything.

3. Track Your Reps: What daily action moves you toward money? How many times did you do it this week?

CHAPTER 8

# PICK LEVERAGE

## *HOW TO GET WHAT YOU'RE WORTH*

I knew a real estate developer named John. He was 12 or 15 years older than me, so he was well into his adult life when I was still a teenager. I never worked for his company, but we did work together—buying properties he owned and getting into some of his developments. And I watched him a lot, studied what he did, and learned from him.

One of the things I learned from John was the importance of leverage, which is the power to build on your hard work to multiply your impact and influence those around you. When you deliver exceptional results or establish yourself as invaluable to a company, that gives you leverage.

You create leverage through your hard work, your network, and the value you provide. Leverage also comes from the goals you attain for yourself, your employer, or your company.

Some people work so hard and do so well that they build leverage without fully realizing it. John was one of those people. He had built a strong real estate development and construction company.

John was very good at developing raw pieces of property, able to visualize how they would be used and how to get more out of them. He knew how to work with towns, town planners, and contractors—and, honestly, everyone. With his engineering background, he also understood site plans, water mitigation, bridge work, and public roads.

But for a long time, he didn't understand how much leverage he had built up.

I remember him having a hard time with a project in a particular town—a 16-lot subdivision for people 55 and older. It seemed like everyone was fighting him on it: the engineering firm, the town lawyer, the town board—every possible obstacle.

His argument for the project was that these individuals would pay taxes but wouldn't add children to the school system, so they wouldn't be a drain on local services. From a services standpoint, they shouldn't have been a big cost to the town.

It wasn't a huge subdivision, but for this town it was fairly significant, and he had another project behind it that was going to be about 100 to 115 units. The town didn't want that influx of people, so nothing seemed to be falling his way.

I was doing a few smaller projects, so I went to a town meeting to speak my piece. I'll never forget John standing up and saying, in front of everybody:

"Listen, it feels like no matter what I do, the town doesn't want this project. As a matter of fact, I feel like my engineer and my attorney aren't really doing the work they should be doing.

"And you know what I've realized? There are a lot of towns that would take an increase in their tax base that is greater than what it would cost them for these people to live here. As much as we all love kids, they cost a lot in terms of the school system, and none of these residents are going to be bringing children. They couldn't bring children even if they wanted to, because it would be a violation of the HOA.

"But I've decided not only to pull this project, but to stop doing work in this town altogether. I can do these projects anywhere. There are over one hundred towns in Connecticut, and I can go to any of them and do a project. So I'm good."

He went on for a while, but it was very well said. I remember the town planner looking at the commission of planning and zoning. The engineer looked at the attorney.

He wrapped up by saying, "I'm very successful, I'm very blessed, but I'm not going to work with people who fight me every inch of the way just because there's been some change on the board."

He smacked everybody upside the head—figuratively, but respectfully—and then he walked out.

John was one of the bigger developers in that area, and there wasn't a lot of development there. If he left, the town planner, engineer, and attorney wouldn't have much to do.

The finance people in town wanted money from their tax base. They wanted revenue. They had been talking in meetings for years about trying to increase the population of folks who did not have small children because they saw the potential for their school system to get overburdened.

It was one of those moments where they realized they didn't have the leverage. John had it, and he had the solution to their problems. When he walked out, you could just feel the air go out of that meeting.

I remember turning to my attorney and saying, "This thing will be approved in a month—these people need him a lot more than he needs them." And that was exactly what happened.

At that time, I wasn't in a position to do something like that myself. But I said, when I have that kind of leverage, this is how I'm going to use it.

About a year later, I asked John why he decided to make that speech. He said, "I asked myself, do I need them more than they need me? Hell no, I don't. Do they need me more than I need them? Hell yes, they do. So I started thinking, why am I negotiating from a position of weakness when the leverage is mine?"

That was a massive lesson for me.

He wasn't a confrontational guy by nature, which made it even more powerful. I think that's also why we got along well. I wanted to confront everybody about everything, always. I think we both enjoyed the differences we had.

I learned a lot from John about diplomacy with leverage. He had it, but he didn't beat people over the head with it. He just said: "Here's the leverage, here's why I have it, here's what happens if we don't do this. I'm going to be fine either way, but I don't think you will be. With all due respect, you need me more than I need you. I like you. I respect you. I like working with you—but not to the detriment of me, my family, and my company."

And I tried to live by that approach as much as I could for as long as I could.

## CREATING PERSONAL LEVERAGE

Leverage is knowing that you provide something to a company, a team, or a situation that complements what's already there. If you can provide something nobody else can—or create high value by being a high performer within a team—you have leverage.

This allows you to get more of what you want, using that leverage to pick the next job or opportunity, and eventually creating your own financial freedom.

When most people take jobs, start a business, or become consultants or salespeople, they're looking to conform. But don't conform—outperform. That creates leverage that eventually leads to financial freedom.

When you're a top performer, no company wants to lose you. No sales team wants to lose its top salesperson. No team wants to lose its most productive asset. Because leaders know that if they can't keep high performers, they can't compete with companies and teams that can.

## COMPANIES ALSO CREATE LEVERAGE

You can use your leverage with a company because that company is also trying to create their own leverage in their marketplace. Every job you've had, they're trying to do what you're trying to do on a larger scale. They're trying to outperform, they're trying to be a higher performer in the industry, they're trying to create more leverage. They can buy products cheaper, charge more, or buy marketing en masse at a better rate. They're trying to do what you're trying to do. So, if you align with them on what they're trying to accomplish, you create leverage.

Once you've created leverage, you need to act on it. You need to start asking for opportunities, promotions, and bonuses.

I've worked at companies where I've created a lot of leverage for myself. Then I went to the people who ran those companies and said, "I'd like to find a way to make additional money. Here's what I'm thinking." And I've had managers, bosses, and business owners say, "Let's talk." Sometimes they've said, "That sounds fair to us. We can provide that." Sometimes they've made a counteroffer.

Of course, some companies will flat out say no. There was a time when my boss said he wouldn't do anything at all for me, even though I was the highest performer at the entire company on both the sales and management side. He would not make any change that would help me make any more money.

Now, if that happens, then you know there's a lid on you. No matter how well you perform, you will be prevented from creating more opportunities for your financial future. In this situation, you need to just move on. That's what I did. When he said no, I left and started my own company.

## SPEAK UP

When you've created leverage, let people know—be vocal. You want your leverage to be visible.

That doesn't mean you run around acting like an idiot, or scream and yell, or diminish what other people are doing. It means you're clear and outspoken about what you provide. Focus on what you're doing and what you're creating. The profitability you generate gives you control of the narrative that describes your work ethic and productivity.

Be willing to point out how productive you've been. When I got into sales, I developed weekly, monthly, quarterly, and annual goals. I would present those goals and detail how I achieved and exceeded them. I'd say, "My goal was to grow EBITDA by 20 percent, and we grew by 34 percent." Or, "My goal was to grow top line by this percentage, and I beat that." Or, "My goal was to unload X packages a minute, and I blew that goal out of the water."

Make sure to ask questions about why you're not making more considering the value you bring: "If you don't mind me asking, why haven't I received the bonuses others have?" "If you don't mind me asking, why am I not on the promotion list?"

If you find yourself at a company where promotions, bonuses, and advancement are based entirely on seniority—and your productivity has no effect—my advice is to find a company where you'll be compensated for being a more productive, high-value employee. That's why I didn't stay long at UPS. It was a purely seniority-based deal. If I outperformed you, but you'd been there longer, you got better routes, better opportunities, and more overtime. I always wanted to work someplace where high performance led to higher rewards. Where was the incentive at UPS to be the best?

When you ask for a raise or promotion, focus not only on what you've done but on the impact it has had on the company. Don't just tell your employer, "I've been here two years. Here's everything I've done. Here's everything I've provided. I'd love to talk about making more money." Do your market research to determine your value. Be able to say, "Here are the things I've done. Here's how they positively impacted the company. Here are the results I've provided. Here's how much money the company has made because of me."

Market research lets you be clear about the proper pay for someone in your position producing at your level. You should be able to say, "My position, on average, pays X. I'm not making that. Here's what companies generally ask of somebody in my position. I will outperform that. As a matter of fact, I'll outperform everyone here, so I don't expect to make the same amount of money as they do."

When you earn bonuses, additional commissions, or increased pay, keep that between you and your boss or supervisor. I never shared what I was making—or not making—with coworkers, because they would only use it against me.

If I was going to interview for a new position, I didn't broadcast it to the entire company. I just waited until it was time and applied. I didn't want to listen to people saying I hadn't been there long enough, or that they were more entitled. I didn't need that noise.

## BUILDING RELATIONSHIPS

It's true what people always say: It's who you know.

Now, a lot of people think that means it's about who you're related to. But that's wrong. It's really about the relationships you create.

When I was getting into real estate, another guy started around the same time. He was about 15 years older and already established in his life. He took off like crazy right away.

I finally said, "Hey, Ed, if you don't mind me asking—you've had massive success. It looks like you got into this business like the rest of us, without much money. So what did you do? What's been the key to your success?"

He said, "You're right. Like the rest of you, my biggest issue was lack of capital. So, before I bought anything, I started going to the small local banks and credit unions in southeastern Connecticut—not the big ones, just the local ones. And I found out I had a family connection to somebody at one of them. Because of that, I got a meeting with the vice president of lending.

"They were looking to do loans in the speculative building space—spec homes, multifamily, all kinds of things I was interested in. I had a meeting with the board, the deal made sense to me, and I secured a line of credit.

"Then I found the cleanest, easiest deal possible, because I knew if I could repay the money fast, I'd gain traction with the bank. I bought a lot in Norwich, built a raised ranch I could finish in six or seven weeks, and sold it quickly. It didn't matter if I made much profit. I just wanted to repay the bank immediately.

"After that, I built relationships with contractors. Instead of hiring them at a fixed rate, I'd show them the total budget and what I'd make. Then I'd say, 'If we can come in under budget at this target price, I'll share some of my profit with you.' If they saved me $12,000 on drywall, and I gave them 10 percent, that was $1,200 to them."

My mind was blown. His relationships didn't just happen—he cultivated them.

Relationships are powerful in any business. When I was a social worker, there was a guy named Mark. Everybody liked him—providers, clients, everybody. His secret? He worked hard to build relationships with the third-party providers. Because of that, his job was 10 times easier than ours.

The same was true later in the waste management business. When an incinerator burned down, my profits were gone—until I called on a relationship I had built five years earlier. That connection saved me tens of thousands and helped me when it came time to sell the company.

Relationship building is everything. The relationships I've built—and the networking I've done—have helped me create financial independence for my family.

## MOST PEOPLE AREN'T BORN WITH VALUABLE BUSINESS RELATIONSHIPS

I wasn't born into any of my business relationships. None of those people were family. None were childhood neighbors. These are people I developed connections with over time—because I went out of my way to build them. And a lot of folks just don't.

One way to do it is by being a great team player. There's nothing better than a high performer who's also a great teammate. Someone who can say, "Here are all the things I've done, but damn, I love my team. The greatest asset we have is our leadership and the people I work with."

The key is to build relationships with the right people—the ones who can get you into the rooms of the decision-makers. That's how you gain access. Look around your company or your network. Are you in the same spaces as the decision-makers? Have you built relationships with the people who make decisions?

You want to be in those rooms, hearing what they're planning, where they're going, and how they're going to grow the business. Be a part of that—and show them how serious you are.

And when you're in those rooms with the right people, keep it professional. If they share something in that room, it stays there.

## BUILD RELATIONSHIPS WITH ACCOUNTABLE PEOPLE

At your company, always look for opportunities to make connections with the right people. Get involved in every aspect of the business. Too many folks just punch the clock, do the least they can, and go home. They have no aspirations to pick money, move up, or create financial independence. Or maybe they once had those aspirations and gave up. But that's not you.

To get the best return on a relationship, look for accountability. People who don't take accountability won't be good long-term partners.

When I interview people, I ask why they left a company or industry. If they say, "It was '08, you know what I mean? The market crashed, everybody failed, what are you gonna do?"—that's a terrible answer.

A great answer is, "I was in real estate when 2008 hit. I wasn't positioned for that. I hadn't diversified enough, I wasn't prepared for a market change, and I was too heavily invested in one end of the market. Because I was unprepared, I got hit harder than others."

That's accountability. Those are the people I want to build with.

And when I say build relationships, I'm not talking about making friends. Too many people confuse the two. They go to company picnics, barbecues, bowling nights—building relationships that aren't profitable.

Ask yourself: Are you looking for more friends, or do you want to make more money for your family? If it's friends, that's fine—but maybe you should go somewhere else. I'm going to treat you well, respect you, and support you, but I'm also going to challenge you to make more money.

You want connections that create a healthy, profitable culture—people with strong work ethics who take accountability. Those are the relationships that will move you forward.

## KEEP AN EYE OUT FOR OPPORTUNITY

To use leverage, you have to be active in both your job and your industry. When I was at the real estate company, I was also active in the real estate community. I was going to these networking events and leadership events. I received training, I networked, and I met people.

The way real estate worked when I started out is the companies had their own leaderboards and information. Everybody worked in a silo, so you didn't know who was good and who wasn't. But when I met people, I would always tell them what I'd done. "I'm the number one agent over there; I made this many transactions last month." Doing this allowed me to build leverage in my industry in the same way that I built leverage in my job.

I kept an eye out for other opportunities to fast-track my goals. When I looked at RE/MAX, I thought—*Wow, look at the marketing, look at the compensation, look at what they're doing to try to create leads.* I could see it would be a good place to move.

Any industry I was in, I studied that industry and I studied my competition. I was looking at what everybody else was doing in the industry. Yes, I built strong relationships with people that were at my company. But from networking and from attending conferences, I built amazing relationships beyond my company.

Those industry connections meant I could be the first one to know about potential opportunities before somebody else got them. Managers and owners I met through networking and at events would call me and say something like, "Hey, man, I don't know if you're looking, but we have this opportunity coming up. We have a head of sales job—full-time commission, and we're also going to pay you this much."

Not every opportunity was the right one for me, but my networking meant I had that first shot.

I was always asking questions about where people I talked to were working. What do they do well? What do they do poorly? What are the three things you like the most about the company? What are the three things you like the least?

I gathered so much intel through networking. I knew what my competition was up to. I knew what people were making. I knew how companies were structured, and what they liked and didn't like. Then I analyzed the information so I could find the places where I was going to compete.

When I got into real estate, I realized that most of the managers or company leaders didn't sell. So I'm like, I'm going to become a great salesperson. I'm good now, but I'm going to be great and have a lot of success.

And then I'm going to be able to teach people to be great salespeople. And then why in the world wouldn't every real estate agent want to work with me? I'm going to be at the top of the leaderboard.

I had all this information on the industry. I could tell you what products they sold. I could tell you their strengths and weaknesses. And I knew how to capitalize on that information to recruit a big team. I knew who was good, and I knew how I could offer them something better than what they had where they were working now. I knew how to take that and say, "I know y'all are structured like this. Here's how we do it where I am."

I figured out everything people didn't like about the industry and their current companies before I started in with my company. I started going through the things they didn't like about lead delivery, management, training, expectations, bonuses, and I started figuring out what I could do differently. So when I came in, I had done enough research for such a long period of time that I knew what people liked and what they didn't like, and I knew how to do it differently.

I knew that it would take discipline to do it differently because it would require sacrificing money. I knew that if I had a crazy-great profit-sharing deal, more than everybody else, it would take me more time to make money. But I had discipline. I didn't need to make it in the next 27 minutes. I had multiple streams of income coming in already.

So I went a couple of years where I just paid myself a very, very, very small salary and put every dollar back into the company. I knew I could do that because I knew the industry well enough to know I was going to make it work.

## UNDERSTANDING LEVERAGING

Look at yourself in the mirror and ask yourself if you can say:

- → I am a high performer.
- → I provide more value than the majority of the people there.
- → These are the things I've done to problem-solve.
- → I've given more than almost everybody else around me has.
- → I'm somebody the company should not want to lose.
- → I've built good relationships with my employer, with my manager, with the investors, and with the consultants.

If you can say those things, then don't be afraid to ask for more. When you're producing more and delivering more value, you should be compensated accordingly.

And if you can look yourself in the mirror and believe all those things, then you should ask for them openly, honestly, and with respect—using the connections you have created. That's how you utilize your leverage to move up, to make more money, and to eventually receive financial freedom.

But not every company will pay you more. What if they recognize your value but won't reward it? Then it's time to go somewhere else, taking your skills, your work ethic, and your track record, and becoming a high performer somewhere that will compensate you appropriately.

In the next chapter, we'll talk about when and how to make that move. Because picking money also means being willing to walk away and rebuild when you've maxed out where you are.

→CHAPTER 8←

# REFLECTION QUESTIONS

1. Document Your Value: Write down everything you've delivered in the past 90 days. Can you prove it with numbers?

2. Ask for More: When's the last time you actually asked for a promotion or raise? If it's been over a year, why?

3. Know Your Number: What would make you walk away from your current job? Write that number down.

CHAPTER 9

# PICK MOBILITY

## *MAKE MOVES, MAKE MONEY*

What happens when you're at a company where you can't grow anymore? You're doing what you need to do. You're providing value, you've got leverage. You're talking about promotions, bonuses, and commissions—but they just won't pay you more.

That's when it's time to make a move. What have you got to lose?

When people don't make those moves, it's because it makes them uncomfortable. Changing jobs is uncomfortable. Changing locations is uncomfortable. Trying to get a promotion can be uncomfortable.

So you have to ask yourself, are you able to make moves that require you to go outside of your comfort zone? If so, then you can go ahead and think about being upwardly mobile and leading yourself to financial freedom. If not, well, you should probably forget about that and just grind on until you die.

If you're not going anywhere, you've got to take a chance on going somewhere else. Don't let the fear of the unknown stop you from making a change for a better opportunity. People will say, well, the grass isn't always greener on the other side, and it's true that you can't really know what will happen in a move. The new opportunity isn't going to be perfect. You might get a new boss you don't like as much. You might say, "Well, I liked my old boss more."

## CHANGING JOBS CAN BE GREAT

People don't change jobs because they're usually afraid the change will make their life worse. Too often they ignore the other possibility—changing jobs can make your life *a lot better.*

Take the case of Scott, a young man who was in my unit when I was working at the State of Connecticut as a supervisor.

Scott was probably 10 years younger than me. I liked him a lot, but he was not a good fit for the job. He was too chaotic, too unfocused, and too unstructured to work for the State of Connecticut with all its rules and regulations.

I was a training supervisor trying to help him navigate that, and I got to a point where I realized I couldn't. It was like trying to fit a square peg into a round hole.

So I sat Scott down one day and asked, "How do you think it's going here, man? You've been here now a year and a half. You made it through your work and test period, but it's really more like two years before you're fully through the tryout period. So, do you think you're going to make it here?"

And you know, I think he wanted to be good at the job because it was his first real job after he got his degree. But I think he knew what I was getting at. I was very direct, like, "Do you enjoy this job?" And he didn't. And he didn't enjoy the stress of working with kids and families, because dealing with abuse and neglect is very stressful.

I knew he took it personally. I knew it bothered him. I knew he struggled with it, and I asked him about it, calling him out.

About four months later, Scott came in and said, "I found a job working outside at a camp. I'm basically running this portion of it. I've got no boss. I make less money, but money's not important to me at all. I just want to make enough to make a living."

Now you might think I should have lectured him. Said he was crazy to be making less money. It's certainly not the advice I'm giving in this book!

But I don't lecture people. A person convinced against their will is never really convinced. And not everyone is driven by the same things.

I saw Scott 10 years after that and asked how it was going.

He said, "Man, I love it out of my mind. I couldn't be happier. I do a few things on the side to make some extra money, but I love my job. I don't miss working at the state. I'm a happy man.

"I make good decisions in my life. Good decisions for my family. I need to be outside. I don't need people telling me what to do. I need to be able to wear shorts and a T-shirt and hang out and do whatever the hell I want all day long. I'm just not good with structure, but I can make it to my job, I don't have a lot of meetings, and I feel like I'm making a difference.

"It's all positive. It's not like dealing with abuse and neglect court cases. These are parents who can send their kids to camp, and I'm going to be there to help—to educate, entertain, and challenge. And I'm wanted there. I've realized that I need to work with people who want to work with me. And what killed me at the state is the people who didn't want to work with me. I couldn't stand that. I didn't want to beg them to work with me."

Now, I'm not saying you should quit your job for one that pays less—that's definitely not the moral of a book called *Pick Money*. I'm just saying that getting caught up in the idea that you can't quit a job because the next one might be worse is dumb. You can't predict the future. And even if the next job is worse, you don't have to stay in that job either. Picking money means making as many moves as you need to make.

## KNOW YOUR PRIORITIES

Scott didn't really know what kind of job he needed until he got it. But if you're reading this book, it's because you know that what you want is to pick money for you and your family. So if you say, "I don't want to leave my job because I like my boss," I ask, "Do you like your boss enough to make 30 percent less?" And if you say yes, then I can't help you pick money because you're picking comfort. You're picking having friends at work. You're picking a network of people.

What you want to do is pick the better opportunity for your family. You say, "Well, there's a company over here that's going to pay me a little bit more than I'm making now, and there's a good opportunity for promotion. These are the different levels I can reach, and they said they'll give me a bonus if I can bring my current volume along with me. That means I'll be making 30 percent more than I'm making here."

It's great to know that you are moving to more opportunities. Even though it was often a tough decision, every time I made a move, I was very excited.

I was very excited for the opportunity to be challenged. I was never nervous about that. I'm fired up by a new opportunity to prove myself to people. To be somebody that the company values. To be a great teammate. To help the company and the people around me grow. That's how I look at it.

Accountable people like to be challenged. My only fear was getting a job that didn't challenge me, let me grow, and allow me to make more money for my family.

I wasn't worried about people thinking, *That guy tries too hard.* It's funny to me that if you do really well at something, people call you a kiss-ass. Bro, I don't kiss ass; I kick ass. I do better than you. I work harder than you. I'm not here to make friends—I'm here to pick money for my family. Think what you like.

When I had a job, the fastest way for me to make more money was to get a new job. After I got my real estate license, I got hired by William Raveis. Then RE/MAX made me an offer, so I took it. Then I took an offer from Coldwell Banker, and I just kept moving. Whenever a company made me an offer, I asked myself—what is the best thing to do for me and for my future family? And if it was a good offer that gave me more growth potential—then I took it.

Most of the time, these jobs didn't provide a ladder of success all the way up. But I made more money at every job I moved to. If they couldn't meet my value, then I was out. Because people need to know you have the courage to make tough decisions and leaps. My leverage was my proven track record of working my ass off for my company and for being a phenomenal team player.

I always made it clear—I will do everything you need me to do, but if I can't move up, if I can't make money for my family, or if I'm not making a fair income, then I'm not afraid to leave.

## LEAVING IS NOT DISLOYAL

When I started in the insurance business, I was working for somebody else and working harder than I had ever worked in my entire life. For five years, I was working at an IMO, which is an Insurance Marketing Organization. But then I started looking around me, and I realized that the company was keeping a lot of money.

So I went to the leadership team there and said, "Hey, I can't keep doing this. We've got to figure out something that's remotely fair, because right now, you are keeping everything, and the rest of us are not making any money."

They said no to making any changes, so I quit and decided to launch my own IMO.

Now, IMOs work with big insurance carriers—household names. They give you the products, you sell their products, and they pay you and all the agents.

One of the guys who worked at one of those huge insurance companies had been there for 20+ years. I was talking to him about how I was planning to structure my IMO, and he asked me, "How do you know your model is going to work better than the model you left?"

And I said, "Well, the model at the company I left was . . . they kept almost all the money. But here, you'll get paid more money because I'm going to share more of the commissions for doing the exact same amount of work. Now, if somebody offered you 30, 40, 50, 60 percent more to do the same exact job somewhere else, wouldn't you quit and go take that higher paying job?"

And he said, "No, I wouldn't." He'd been working at his company for more than 20 years, and he couldn't see any way he'd ever leave.

A lot of people say stuff like this. They've become more loyal to their company than they are to the needs of their own family.

But a year and a half later, when another company offered him a job with better pay, the guy quit his old job and went for the new one.

You might wonder why he changed his mind. Why, in less than two years, did he go from "I would never quit" to "I quit"?

Well, even though I beat him over the head about it, I'm not going to take the credit. When it's hypothetical, it's easy to say no. But once it became a real situation, that's very different. Once he had this new opportunity, and he had to look at his wife and kids and consider their future, he started asking himself, "Why can't I make more at the company?"

Loyalty has its place. And it's worth seeing if the place you've been with can match where you want to go. My advice, after he got the offer, was to ask his current company to give him more money, matching the offer. Maybe they won't offer the 35% increase you have lined up elsewhere. Maybe they offer a 22% bump. You could choose to stay for that if you wanted. You'd still be ahead of where you were.

When he went to that company and asked for a raise, they said flat out that they were not going to give him any more money. He got frustrated. And when he was frustrated, he became emotional. And when he became emotional, he made the decision to take the new opportunity.

Rejection can make us tremendously powerful.

When we're rejected and we take our anger and use it to our benefit, we can do some amazing things. His anger created the courage for him to quit his job and go to a completely different company with a new set of people.

He's been there for more than five years doing the same work for a hell of a lot more money for his family. And he says he couldn't be happier.

So you should always be open to change. For you, and for your family. Your loyalty needs to be picking money, not picking your company.

Not every change is good, though. Leaving a job you've been at for 20 years to join a start-up that winds up going out of business in six months isn't a good decision for your family. So it's important to think about how stable the opportunity you're considering actually is.

You also have to be happy with your decision. That doesn't mean you have to have a job that makes you happy; it just means you need to know who you are and how your work situation affects your happiness.

Some people can work a job they hate, go home, and truly disassociate from that job. They may not like the job, or the people, but when they punch out at five, they're good. It doesn't bother them. They're not stressed out.

That's how things are with me. I was there to do a job. When I left, I left it all behind me.

But that's me. It may not be you. So, even when picking money, you have to make sure to pick a situation that matches what you want for you and your family. If you're miserable and upset 24/7, chances are that won't be good for your family. If you're the kind of person who carries the job home with you—and there's nothing wrong with that—it better be the right job.

## KNOWING WHEN TO LEAVE

Every year, you need to check where you stand against your 20% growth income goal, or whatever you've set your goal to be. If you're falling short, it's time to advocate for yourself, and to also consider moving to your plan B. If you've been at the company three to five years, and you want to grow your income by 20% every year but that isn't happening, then plan B is whatever change you're going to make to meet that annual growth goal.

I've had a lot of jobs, and I've left a lot of jobs, but those jobs have never left me. They always wanted me to keep working there. I was productive. I did all the right things. But if they weren't giving me what I needed, I had to go somewhere new.

So let's say you're analyzing your income year over year, realize that you were making eighty grand a year when you started, and four years later you're up to eighty-four grand. You aren't getting any extra bonuses or commissions, so there's just nothing else you can get. There's no future in where you are. There's no promotion in sight, and nobody will even talk to you about it. Now, you should start networking, gaining intel, and building relationships. You can figure out your industry and also show people you have the courage to go ahead and make a move if you need to.

Start interviewing at least three months in advance to cement your move. Interview for jobs you might not even take. If you haven't interviewed for a while, just take the interview for practice.

## DON'T MAKE ENEMIES

Everything you do, bad or good, can come back to you. Every interaction you have can have an effect on your future.

I've said before, I used to drink a lot when I was young. If you and me were at a bar, and you were a dude who looked at me the wrong way, I'd probably want to fight you—I was out of control. One time I got into a physical altercation with a group of guys at a bar called Hot Shots in Willimantic in a parking lot across the street. It was a few of my buddies against a bunch of those guys, and we ended up on the right side of it, and they ended up on the wrong side. But we all got arrested, so I guess we were all on the wrong side of it.

A year and a half later, I was 20 years old and just about to graduate from college. I went to one of the casinos in Connecticut, hoping to do an internship in the casino's marketing department.

And at the casino, there was this guy I remembered from that fight. He was a little older than me and kind of an important guy there. He was part of the interview process. He said, "Do you remember me?" And I was like, "I think so."

I knew there was no way I was getting that job. And I remember thinking to myself, *I'm accountable for every single thing I do and don't do in my life, and those things can affect my future employment.* It wasn't the end of the world, but it was a good opportunity a friend of mine had referred me to that I wasn't getting. And it was a good lesson.

Now, not everyone you fight is going to decide years later whether you get a job. But there's a very good chance that if you leave a company or a job, you may find yourself interacting with that old boss or a coworker sometime in the future.

So always exit your current job professionally and leave on good terms. Do not burn any bridges because the world is a smaller place than you think it is. You have no idea who will be sitting across the desk from you one day, be on your team, or be part of some board of directors. You never know who you're going to encounter again.

When I was in real estate, I left my first real estate company after six months. My manager was much older—she was in her 60s or 70s, and I was in my early 20s. And I remember leaving, and she wanted me to do an exit interview kind of deal. And I talked very highly of her and the company, the people. I said, listen, this RE/MAX company has very aggressive marketing, they have a different structure, and I'm going to give it a shot.

After about a year and a half, the company, William Raveis, wanted to recruit me back. They said, "We've seen how successful you are, and we would love for you to come back to the original office you were in because, frankly, they could use some help, sales-wise, and you sell quite a bit of real estate. Would it be a problem for you to go back there?"

And I said, "Absolutely not—why would it be? Did you ask the manager?"

They said, "Yes. They have no problem taking you back."

The recruiter, who was one of the upper-level management people in New England, said it was unusual, because once people leave, they either don't want to go back to the office, or they're not welcome back. And I told him, I respect your company, I respect the people that work there. There are some things I want to do differently, certainly, but you guys have a great company with great people.

I always leave in good standing. I speak well about the company, and they speak well about me. And if one of those men or women ends up somewhere else in a job where they have decision-making ability, or they're a C-level executive, now all of a sudden, they're like, "Yeah, I know Shawn. He worked here and did great for us. He worked with us for four years, but there was just more he wanted to do, and he didn't think he could achieve it with us, so he left to pursue that opportunity."

With all the companies I worked at, there was only one opportunity where I left, and they went after me with everything they had. It was a big organization, and I left and started my own company. A lot of their people came with me, which the organization did not take too kindly to.

They sued me for years, and I defended myself with everything I had. It's a fight they probably shouldn't have picked.

After all that, when I ended up selling my insurance distribution company, one of the first people I referred over to the parent company that acquired me was the guy that had sued me. Life's just too short, and business isn't personal.

## DON'T LET THEM GET IN YOUR HEAD

So, every once in a long while you may have a situation where the company is going to hold a grudge. When you're in sales and you leave a company, if you've done really well people will threaten to sue you. Mostly they won't, but sometimes they'll follow through on that.

It may never happen, but if it does, don't let it stop you.

When I went through litigation, the rule I had with the guys who were working with me and were getting sued was: We're not going to talk about it. If the attorney needs something, I'll talk to him.

But we're all not going to talk about it, because people sue you to emotionally paralyze you. And we're not going to let these individuals do that to us. So we just kept it moving, and we stayed focused on what we could control.

That's when I realized that big can sometimes try to bully small. But I was like, I'm just going to stay the course. No matter what happens, I'm going to stay the course. And I think that, at the end of the day, it really allowed me to grow immensely as a businessman. All this other stuff was going on, and I just kept moving, we kept growing, we kept becoming profitable.

And while we were doing that, we didn't talk about them. We didn't talk about where we came from, we didn't talk about them negatively, we didn't discuss it in any way at all.

When people are trying to get under your skin and they can't, it messes them up. They get spun up about you, so they're talking about you every minute of every day. And when your enemies make mistakes, you don't want to get in their way.

As a matter of fact, the best marketing you'll ever have is from your competition. The guys I've competed against have been my best marketers.

"Don't work with Shawn," they'll say. "I'm warning you. Here are the reasons."

And people are like, "I didn't even know who he was until you told me about him!" And then they want to check me out because they think it's weird that someone is going out of their way to say, "Don't work with that guy." They think, *That is odd because I'm an adult, and I'm an independent person, and you're adamant that I shouldn't work with him. If he wasn't any good, I wouldn't even be thinking about working with him. So why are they bringing him up? Let me check him out and see what he does.*

So, for all of you who have competed against me, allegedly, even though my number's been a lot larger than yours, thank you for the free marketing that you provided as you negatively talked about me all the time. Thank you for running meetings about why not to join my company, which then pushed people over to my company. For that, I am eternally grateful.

What I'm saying is, almost all the time, if you leave professionally, the company will act professionally. Companies understand that it's okay to stand up for yourself, to use leverage, make moves, and want upward mobility. They'll respect someone who is determined to get paid what they deserve, as long as they do it professionally, honestly, and directly. And if they don't, you can still come out the winner. So, when you see it's time to move, *move*!

→CHAPTER 9←

# REFLECTION QUESTIONS

1. The Stuck Test: Yes or no—can you grow in the career or job you have now? If not, why are you still there?

2. Fear Versus Reality: What's the worst that happens if you change jobs? Write that down. Now write down what happens if you don't.

3. Map Your Exit: If you had to leave your job in 90 days, where would you go? Start researching that now.

CHAPTER 10

# PICK FOCUS

## *THE POWER OF ENDURANCE*

Society tells people that if they're going to become an upper-level professional, like a doctor, a lawyer, or a CEO, it's okay to work a hundred hours a week in pursuit of that. It's okay to sleep in the office. It's okay to be away from your family most of the time. It's okay to make those sacrifices.

If you tell someone you're a first-year medical resident and work 80 hours a week and get so little sleep you're running off fumes and barely see your family and live off ramen noodles and are tired all the time, no one thinks, *That's weird—why are they doing that?* They say, "Good for you, working hard to build your career as a doctor."

If the CEO of a major corporation has an article about them describing how they work 12-hour days and weekends and are obsessed with productivity, people say, "Now that's the way to succeed in the corporate world."

But when people looked at me working as an employee, or as someone running a business, they would say, "What do you mean you work seven days a week, fourteen hours a day? That's horrible! Why are you working these crazy hours?" To which I'd reply, "What do you mean? Doctors do this all the time. They just work and sleep and study. Just because I have a sales job, now all of a sudden working like this is wrong? Is it wrong to work those hours so I can have my own sales team or build my own company?" And they would reply, "But they're *doctors*! Of course they have to do that!"

The goal of financial freedom—when divorced from a prestige job—is looked down upon by society. You run into somebody, and they ask,

"What does your son do?" "Oh, he's in medical school." "Oh my God, he's in *medical school*?"

There's this sense that, my God, that medical student is just a better person than us.

But if they ask, "What does your boy do?" and you reply, "He's in sales," they're likely to respond, "Oh, okay, whatever. Guess it pays the bills."

Listen, I want good doctors. We need good doctors and good attorneys. And in our society, we accept that doctors or lawyers will work long hours. Tell someone a doctor is working 100 hours a week, and no one will bat an eye. People say, that's just what you have to do. But for other jobs and professions, it is seen as insane to work so many hours. But why can't people accept that this is just what you have to do to build a business as well?

## WORK LIKE A DOCTOR

If you're trying to become financially free, or you're picking money, then society will tell you that you're wrong to work so much, even if that doctor makes $200,000 their first year and you make $700,000. But who gives a shit?

Now, I've never cared what society thinks, but other people do. So, if you pick money, you have to be prepared for a lot of people to start second-guessing your choices. Instead of listening to them, you need to develop tunnel vision.

My baseball coach used to tell me, "In football, you can't really hear the crowd because you have a helmet on. So fans don't really bother you much. But in baseball, you can hear people. If I'm playing third base, I can hear what the fans are saying. So don't have rabbit ears. Tuck in your ears, and whatever they say, who cares? Don't listen to it, Shawn. Don't pay attention."

And I never paid attention to it. I was like, "I don't know why he keeps saying this to me; he should be talking to everybody else." Because what the fans said didn't hurt me. I kind of wanted them to say stuff to motivate me. I'm better off when you're talking shit to me than when you're quiet.

But if you're not motivated by everyone telling you that you're wrong, then you need tunnel vision. You can't listen to other people when you have tunnel vision.

Remember, you're working so that your life will be your own. The commitment, the goals, the grind—all this is an exercise in endurance. And if you can't continue to submit to the grind and have endurance, you will regress.

## BUILD A SUPPORT SYSTEM

So how do you endure that grind? Honesty, alignment, and discipline.

Build your support system, because you can't do this on your own. Now, when the shit hits the fan, and you're having a bad day, then yes, that's on you—you've got to figure it out. But for you to achieve your ultimate goals, you can't get there on your own. You need people around you that are true ride-or-die people.

Think about who is in your life. Now write down the names of the people who are pulling for you even if your success doesn't benefit them. The people who, if you become successful, wouldn't gain financially from it. They aren't expecting you to share the money with them. You didn't borrow money from them that they're desperate to get back. They haven't invested in your business. They're not an in-law who wants you to have money to support their daughter. Your financial success will not impact them at all. But they're still pulling for you.

How many of those people do you have in your life? Count carefully and don't lie to yourself. You probably only need one hand. Don't count the people who say they're for you and yet are always negative about what you do or are trying to pull you away from what's important.

It's important to have people like that who you know you can trust. I've always played my cards really close to the vest. I don't discuss my business with people I don't know—why would I feed people the ability to hurt me and my business? But you want to have just a few people you can open up to. Mentors and friends you can talk ideas through with. And I have that.

## BE TRANSPARENT

I often talk to people who are working a full-time job plus another part-time job, and they're like, "So-and-so"—their friend, their spouse—"is frustrated with me. They don't understand me at all."

And I'm like, "Okay, but do they actually, number one, even know what you're doing? Are you honest about that? Have you explained it to them? Have you had a discussion about what you're trying to do?"

And I'm blown away when they say, "Well, no, I don't really want to talk to them about it. I've got to wait and see if I'm successful first."

And I'm like, "Wow, you don't even believe in you."

They're so afraid to lose their friends' validation and high opinion. I was talking to people who went into the same business, working at different places, and they didn't know. They went into the same business and didn't tell each other, or anybody in the family. They were hedging their bets in case it didn't work out.

So I wish they would just be confident enough in themselves to say, "Here's what I'm doing." Because, otherwise, of course they don't understand. If you're going to be hiding it, just don't get in the business. If I go, "Hey, what team should I bet on?" And you're like, "Oh, I don't really know," then I'm not going to take your advice. Same thing if you don't bet on yourself.

Anytime you leave a job to do something different from what people typically do—anytime you become an independent contractor, open a business, or do anything where you're going from a W-2 to a 1099—people around you will have a lot of thoughts. And they'll offer a lot of advice, whether or not it's solicited.

Seriously, if you're going to be in business, man, buckle up because even if you're doing well, and you're talking to people who aren't doing well, they're still going to judge what you do, no matter what.

Because of that, a lot of people are uncomfortable to share what they do. So they avoid it. Their uncle's like, hey, what are you doing now? And they're like, nothing new. Because they're going to be judged and they don't want their uncle to go, "You know, that sounds dumb. You can't make any money doing that."

So they're afraid of being judged. People are thinking, *If I tell my wife or my husband I'm working on this new thing and it totally fails, then I'll look like a fool in front of them.* But the thing is, we're all human beings. We all have successes and failures. It's okay to let others in.

If you don't tell your wife, that just means she doesn't get to pull for you or try to support what you're doing. You're married. Let that mean something. Let the support that's there do the work it's supposed to do.

Going through life every day thinking, *I better not tell anybody—I might fail,* is a miserable existence. And if you don't fail, then sooner or later you're going to have to tell people you had this big secret because you thought you were going to fail. That's going to be miserable too.

Letting the people in who can support you is crucial. But independence has its place, too, mainly in knowing how to tune out all the people with an opinion they don't have the right to have. They aren't the ones running your business. And you're not paying them for consulting advice.

To handle drawing this boundary, I role-play scenarios with people. If you were to say to me, "Hey, you know what I think about your business?" I'd go, "I didn't ask you."

"Hey, Shawn, you know what I was thinking about what you do?"

"Hey, bro, keep your opinion to yourself."

"Hey, Shawn, I was going to give you some advice."

"Well, I don't want advice from a guy who's not where I want to be."

The minute my family members started giving me opinions on things, which they didn't do for very long, I was very clear with all of them that, while I'm not better than any of them, I want more financially than what any of them have.

Be 100% transparent and communicative to your friends and family about what your life's going to be like in the next five years. When I decided to pick money, I was very clear with the mother of my kids. I didn't explain my financial plans to my kids then—my oldest was two at the time—but as they got old enough, I was very honest with them about how hard I was going to work, why I'm working so hard, and what results I want for them for today, tomorrow, and for their future. And I told them that I expect them to continue the way I am, and do even more than I'm doing, because they're more talented. They'll have a great foundation from what they've learned while watching me.

So, if I start a new business on Thursday, I'll tell you about it on Friday. "Man, here's what I'm doing. If I don't make it, I don't make it, but I'm going to give it hell."

Don't hide from it. And if people judge you, well, so what? Who cares? Just remember, it's always okay to say to people, "Hey, bro, I didn't ask your opinion."

## ALIGN YOUR LIFE

All components of your life should be in alignment. Your support system. Your personal goals. And, if you're working a job, your company or your boss's goals.

Everything you do should be in service of picking money. If you need to relocate for a job, all three elements must be aligned. Your family has to be okay with it. You need to be getting a promotion that increases your financial gain. You must meet the needs of your company by relocating. Then it's great. Let's go.

If your family refuses to move, even though it's a big pay bump for you, then you're out of alignment. If you're moving out of state for your job, but the position is a lateral move, that's not in alignment with your personal goals.

I've had people ask me to relocate, and I always ask, "Okay, what does my family get out of it?" And they say, "Well, we need more people here." And I'll reply, "I'm the highest performer you've got. You think I'm going to up and move my family for the exact same job, and the exact same pay? You have lost your mind. I'm frustrated that you even asked me."

It's your job to keep each component in balance so that everything works in harmony. This is part of personal discipline.

Discipline is essential when building your financial security. If you know people who have made a bunch of money, and you see they party too much, drink too much, or get high too often, I promise you that they weren't doing that on their way to making all that money. I mean, if they inherited the money, that's a whole other thing, but we're not talking about those people. If someone just hands you an insane amount of money, you may never need much discipline. But that's the 1%. Anyone who wasn't handed a barrel of money at birth, but has a barrel of money now, had discipline while filling that barrel.

People appreciate people who are disciplined in their goals. If I come to a meeting at 8 AM after going to the gym at 5 AM, they don't think, *Oh my God, I wonder how much he can bench-press.* They think, *He's committed. He's a hard worker. He's focused. He's on the grind.*

## WATCH YOUR HEALTH

Part of that discipline is keeping your mind and body in order. I work out seven days a week to take care of my mind and my body, in that order of importance. Because, yes, I want to be in decent shape. I sure as hell want to be in good health. I want to look good. But also, when I work out, I feel good. And if I feel good, I look good. So feeling good has a lot of power.

You need to keep your mind clear and balanced by doing things to calmly unwind and de-stress. What do most people do? Drink and get high. But as you're moving up, the more things you put into your body that mess you up, keep you from being alert, and lead you toward making bad decisions, the more you are impeding your ability to have financial freedom.

Fortunately, you can also unwind and de-stress by staying fit. You want more energy; you want to feel better. Make exercise and nutrition a part of your everyday life. You don't need to be a gym rat, but stay healthy so you're operating at your sharpest and best throughout your five-year climb.

## WATCH OUT FOR NEGATIVE INFLUENCES

I was working for a life insurance company, and I would speak at what are called "business opportunity meetings." I'd fly into a city and run a meeting in a hotel conference room where anybody who wanted to come in and hear about what we were doing could. I would explain what the company was doing and look to recruit people into the business. There might be 8 people in the hotel conference room or there might be 450.

All sorts of people would show up, some who maybe shouldn't have. I did a meeting one time in Tampa, Florida, and the guys came in wearing flip-flops and drinking beers. I turned to the guy running the meeting and I said, "Dude, who are these people? They got no socks on, no shoes on. They got a beer in their hands. This is a business meeting."

So, one day I was doing a meeting in California. I had a young man I was working with, and I was really just beginning to get to know him. We were getting ready to start the meeting, and we were all in the bathroom because it was going to be a four-hour meeting. I was washing my hands when I saw the young man. He was with another guy who he introduced as his dad.

I'd been sober for a while at that time, but when you've smoked weed 10,000 times, which I have in my lifetime, you're pretty sensitive to the smell. And this guy's dad had clearly just been smoking. So I said, "Cool, good to meet you," and then after a minute I told him, "Hey, man, you can't go in there. We're running a real meeting here. You're high as a fucking kite, and I can't have you in the meeting.

"Your son, who's young, really wants this opportunity to work, and he's got a lot of guys he's recruited in there, and then we're going to be talking about the business. And listen, dude, you can get as high as you want whenever you want—that ain't got nothing to do with me. I'm not judging anybody. But it's not appropriate for you to get high and be at this meeting."

They got upset, of course. It drove a wedge between me and this young man for a period of time. I didn't blame him. But I had to be honest. I told him, "I've been there. I had family members when I was eighteen, nineteen, twenty show up around me, and, dude, no offense—they weren't trying to pull me up. They were trying to pull me down. You're just getting into business, you're trying to create good habits yourself, and it wasn't appropriate to have your dad in the meeting like that. I was just looking out for you."

So, after we'd been in business together about a year, he said, "Hey, man, I want to talk to you about what happened that day. I want to apologize."

I said, "You don't owe me an apology. You were frustrated because that's your father. And I don't owe you an apology either. I was just being direct and honest."

"I realized what you were doing, and I thank you for your honesty," he said. "I know you really care about me because that could have jeopardized our relationship."

"Yeah, but when you're helping people, you don't think about yourself. You just have to shoot them straight," I said. "If that means they're mad at you, they take it out on you, that you jeopardize your relationship, that sucks, it's not fun, but that's what mentorship and leadership are about."

I think that if I was willing to get uncomfortable and stick up for that young man, then he'd be willing to get uncomfortable and stick up for himself. I know that if I'm direct with people, and I'm doing the best that I can, I'm never going to worry about how I say it or what I say. Even if it doesn't work out, I won't second-guess myself if I'm trying to protect someone from the bad habits of their past that are going to bring them down.

## CUT THE DEAD WEIGHT

I see so many people who talk to other people who do nothing but breathe literal death into them, but they still keep talking to them. They listen to them, take advice from them, and communicate with them regularly.

You need to identify the people and things that don't support you and cut them out of your life. Because you can't do what you need to do while the wrong people are pouring poison in your ear.

I don't mean sacrificing like they're dead to you. But if you have a family member or a friend who doesn't believe in anything that you're doing, and all he or she does is waste your time, they are dead weight in terms of your goals. It doesn't mean that they're not your friend or family member anymore. But you just don't have time to communicate with them right now.

When you become financially free, then maybe you'll want to make time to talk to them again, but right now you ain't got that time. You just don't.

Negative people aren't the only dead weight you need to cut out. You also have to look at unnecessary expenses. While you are grinding to pick money, spend only the money that you need to spend, not what you just want to spend. Save more, spend less. Anything you can cut will strengthen you in building your financial freedom. When you get to a certain point, you can start spreading that money around, but you've got to stay lean and mean on your way there.

Cutting out everything that doesn't support you takes intestinal fortitude. But remember, this is short-term sacrifice for long-term gain. Sacrifice during your five-year goal, and later, you'll be able to do a hell of a lot more of what you want. Maybe all of what you want.

Remind the people around you who are involved in your life what's going to happen in five years, that, "Hey, guys, we can live wherever we want then. We can travel. We can make more memories with our families. We'll be in a financial position to take better care of our health. The sky will truly be the limit for us as it pertains to our financial security."

When you've done this, as I have, then your family and your friends will forgive you for your temporary absence. They will undoubtedly thank you when they can live a life where they're no longer held hostage by money—where your financial freedom means you can provide opportunities for them, for the family, and for your community. They will be so proud of you and see that the time and the fun that you sacrificed for a few years was well worth a lifetime of financial freedom.

→CHAPTER 10←

# REFLECTION QUESTIONS

1. Cut the Dead Weight: Are there activities, people, or obligations in your life that are making picking money harder? Name three.

2. Work Like a Doctor: If working 80 hours a week for five years meant financial freedom, would you do it? Write yes or no. Then write why.

3. Remind Yourself Why: What will five years of sacrifice buy you? Write that down and put it somewhere you'll see it daily.

CHAPTER 11

# PICK ACCOUNTABILITY

*ASSESS, ADJUST, ACCELERATE*

In chapter 4, we worked on setting a five-year plan. But that's not the only plan you need to set. You need to have daily, weekly, monthly, quarterly, and annual goals in addition to that five-year goal. A lot of folks will only set five-year plans, thinking they can just avoid dealing with today and count on everything being on track five years later. But you need more than a destination—you need a plan for exactly how you're going to get there.

Once you start on the path toward consistently picking money, you need to consistently work to hold yourself accountable along the journey.

For example, when I was working in a real estate company, they told me I needed to close a million dollars in transactions per quarter to retain my commission level. But I thought to myself, *Well, that's nothing. That's about $333,000 a month, and my average transaction is $300,000, so that's just one house a month.* That didn't work for me.

So I decided, all right, here's what I need to do. I'll take what they say as a base that I can reverse engineer in order to set my goals to be much larger than theirs.

Let's say I want to do a million dollars a month. That's $3 million a quarter, $250,000 a week. That's where I started. That means $12 million in transactions annually.

My manager at the time was a super nice lady who said, "That seems a little bit out of reach. You're just getting started. Why don't you make your goals more attainable and achievable?"

But I told her that, for me, those were attainable and achievable goals. Here's what I'm going to do with my marketing. Here's how much time I'm going to spend on cultivating leads. Here's what I'm going to do with my activity.

Marketing at that time was all billboards, newspapers, and signage. I was very focused on getting listings in areas that had a high traffic count. I put signage everywhere in high traffic areas. You couldn't drive around in southeastern Connecticut without seeing my face.

Then I got rabidly focused on my market advantage—why would you use me as an agent versus everybody else? A lot of folks don't think about that, but you have to understand your market advantage and what drives them to work with you so you can drive their decisions your way. And if I started thinking about that from a goal-oriented standpoint, I knew I would be more successful.

I realized that my market advantage was that I was the only real estate agent who would be ridiculously honest with you about the value of the property you're selling, buying, or renting.

What most real estate agents did was they went out to meet with a client, then gave them the appraisal of their CMA, which stands for Comparative Market Analysis. This is a computer program that calculates the value of a property. You just put the address of the property in, and it does everything for you. It looks at all the factors—square footage, if it's a commercial or a residential property, bedrooms, bathrooms, location, acreage—and tells you what the property can sell for. It's not that complicated.

It's the same program the bank's going to use, the appraiser's going to use, the loan officer's going to use. Because you need the comps when somebody's borrowing the money, unless they're going to pay cash. So none of us are guessing. You wind up with a comprehensive 50-page report that you can show a client and just say, here's what it's worth.

So agents all know what they can realistically get for a property. But then the client—who was always emotionally attached to their property—would think it was worth more. Because *every* client thinks their home is worth more than it is. And instead of pushing back, most agents would just list it at whatever the client wanted, knowing that there would have to be a series of price reductions before the property would be listed at a salable price.

So my idea was that I would always be very, very direct, honest, and transparent about the numbers. I would never let you screw yourself up. I was going to shoot you straight and never allow you to lead us down a path of destruction. I would not just show them the CMA; I would be clear that I was not going to let them waste their time trying to sell at some ridiculous price.

The devil's in the details—the money that I got for my clients, the shorter sales period, the responsiveness of buyers, the marketability of their house. I wasn't going to sell it for too little, but I wasn't going to list it for too much. My goals would be attainable because of my market advantage. You cannot decide to do what everybody else is doing and then set aggressive goals.

I pitched all of that—the whole plan—to my manager, and she still didn't understand it. But I started hitting those new goals right away. In fact, I exceeded them exponentially.

I've created a habit of setting aggressive goals and hitting them most of the time. Not all the time, but most of the time—enough that I have a great success rate.

## BUILDING SUCCESS BY DROPPING THE BULLSHIT

I had that great success rate because I did exactly what I said I would do. And I'll give you an example to show you how effective a solid strategy combined with clear goals can be.

A classmate from high school asked me to take a look at his mother's listing for a small strip mall she was selling in Montville, Connecticut. She had it listed for $1.3 million, but it wasn't selling.

So I ran the numbers for her, and the next day told her, "I have great news for you—I know why it's not selling. It's because it's worth $850,000. So my question is, why did the agent listing this for you put it at $1.3? Because that's a delusional number. I'm really mad that they would steer you wrong like this. Let's call them right now and ask them about it."

I did that sort of thing a lot.

Once the agent was on the phone, I said, "I'm sitting here with Mary, and she wants to know why you misled her by claiming she could sell her property for $1.3 million when it's worth $850,000 at most. Why are you bullshitting her?"

Then I waited.

Charles denied misleading her, and Mary tried to defend him by saying she had suggested the $1.3 million figure and the agent had gone with it. But I told her, "That's no excuse. You're not the professional; he is. He is supposed to give you proper guidance."

Then I said, "Charles, I think we're done here," and I hung up.

Now, as you can imagine, the agents didn't love this. But I was fine with that, because I was establishing my authority and credibility with Mary.

I told Mary, "You're never going to sell it at $1.3. But when your agreement with that agent ends, I'll list it for you. But, Mary, I won't list it at $1.3 million. If you want to list it at $900,000, I'll do it. But not a dollar more. If I were a buyer, I wouldn't pay more than $725. It's a soft market. But I'm willing to start at $900 if you want."

When a client says they want to list a property at $1.3, many agents are too weak, too stupid, and too lazy to say no, even though they know they'll have to keep backing down from that number until they get the sale.

Think about how much work that is. After 60 days, you go back to Mary and say, hey, Mary, we need to drop the price. And they do that maybe seven more times before they get to what the property's worth—before they start listing it at a number they can actually get. So they burn a year or more before they reach the price they should have begun with. And then it sells, because then it's priced realistically.

When a seller insists on an unrealistic price, you have to have the strength to walk away. If someone says they're going to list at $1.2 million, I'm willing to say, "Hey, listen, just call me when your house doesn't sell. It's worth nine hundred grand, and I'd love to sell it for you, but I'm not going to waste our time trying to get $1.2 for this. So just give me a call when you realize you're never going to get what you're asking for now, and I'll come back and sell your property."

And people would call me. Six months later, they'd call and say, "We should have listened to you. We're on a third price reduction, and we're getting nowhere."

If you won't take charge, and you won't walk away, then you can wind up with a list of a couple dozen properties that aren't selling. Agents confused activity with profitability. They'll be like, "Hey, I have twenty-seven listings." And I'm like, "Yeah, but you can't sell any of them."

Why would I want to list 27 properties that can't sell? I would look really inefficient, really inadequate. Nobody would want to work with me.

If you're looking up real estate agents, you should always look at their listings and see what their average ADOM is. ADOM is Average Days on Market. So, number one, you want to see how many they have sold in the last 12 months. Number two, how many they have sold of this particular kind of property. And number three, how long it takes them to sell something.

Because of my ADOM, I started getting more listings than you can imagine.

I never had anything on the market that was on there for six, nine, twelve, eighteen months. Other realtors will say, well, it takes a while.

But no, not when you price it right. Things don't sell when they're not priced right.

Calling an agent and grilling them in front of a potential client is way more effective than having a conversation behind their back. So I would always say, let's call that dude right now.

It's a great thing to do because Mary watches me rake this guy over the coals, and she thinks, *I want Shawn to negotiate for me when I'm selling my strip mall. Because if he's going to negotiate this hard with my realtor, what's he going to do with an opposing realtor?*

I sold Mary's strip mall for just what I said it was worth, $850,000. But as I told Mary, I wouldn't have recommended paying that much for it. I think the buyer overpaid because it was kind of a beaten-up deal. And they probably wouldn't have paid that much if the buyer's agent had done their job.

Because after we closed, the buyer called me. There were tenants in the mall who had stopped paying rent. Now, these tenants had always been sketchy, skating in and paying rent in cash at the last second, but we didn't lie about anything. The buyer's agent just never asked for the rent rolls, which would have told her where all the businesses were with the rent and let her identify any issues.

So I told the buyer, "It's not my job to give any information you don't ask for. I have a responsibility to my client, and a responsibility not to lie, but I don't have a responsibility to volunteer information. I did my job, your agent didn't do her job, and, outside of that, I don't know what to tell you."

So what I did was exactly the strategy I had laid out for my manager. She couldn't see it at the time, but it worked out just the way I thought it would. And all it took was recognizing that there was a way of selling real estate that was better than the way most agents were doing it.

## PICK MONEY, NOT RECOGNITION

What a lot of folks do in business is make the mistake of doing things for the recognition, not for the financial result. This means that they're tricked into doing things that don't benefit them.

Their boss will say, "Tim, if you do A, B, C, and D, you're going to become an Emerald Level. You're going to be on the Fly-High Team. You're going to be at the Million Dollar Round Table."

Who gives a shit? What am I getting paid? I never, ever sought recognition over the financial result for my family. Never. That's when folks achieve goals for the wrong reasons.

My goals were financially driven because I had to provide for my family. I had to provide for the people I was responsible for. Therefore, I focused less of my attention on recognition.

Keep in mind that companies tend to set performance levels that are good for them if achieved but aren't as good for you. I've never wanted to be part of a company like that, and I never wanted to run a company like that.

## GIVE YOUR DECISIONS BREATHING ROOM

Jim was a guy who worked at my company, but not in my agency or on my team. He was a peer. One day, after we'd both been working there for a couple of years, he said, "I want to talk to you about the results I'm getting."

Now, I knew that, to say the least, Jim wasn't crushing it. I knew his numbers weren't good because he was never on the leaderboards. But I didn't know why. I had never looked at his business, because it wasn't any of my business. I didn't know his manager, but his whole team wasn't doing a lot, so I didn't think that he was getting great mentorship or instruction. But it could also be that he was getting good instruction and just wouldn't take it.

So he sat down with me that day, and he showed me everything he did. I was looking at his P&Ls, his expenses, his income, and what bothered me about his business is, he was making decisions too quickly.

I started asking him questions. "Hey, this lead source has been good for me. Why aren't you doing it? It looks like you did it for eight weeks. Why'd you stop?" And he's like, "Well, it was eight weeks."

Then I said, "What about this recruiting deal? It's done really well for a lot of people."

"Well, I tried it for a month, man. It didn't work."

I was like, "All right, what about this thing? You've been doing this thing for fourteen months and it hasn't worked. Why are you still doing it?"

"I don't know. It's somebody I know."

So, after we get done going over this whole thing, I said, "Jim, do me a favor. I'm going to lay out a blueprint of what you should do. You're going to give it ninety days."

I told Jim that, in business, you've got to give something time to breathe. Like, you might've been killing it with the leads for two months, but you didn't make any sales. So you think, this isn't working. But it's also real estate. Our average contract to close is like 62 days. So how do you even know whether it's working? You don't. This isn't like playing baseball and you swing the bat, and you hit the ball or you don't. This is like training for baseball, where if you start a new training regimen, and two weeks later you don't see amazing results, well, it's only been two weeks, so of course you don't. You have to give things enough of a chance to know if they'll succeed.

What's the time period where you'll see the pinnacle of your results? Is it 90 days? Is it 120? Is it 62 days? It could be any of those. But it's not two weeks. Jim had done this for a couple of years. And every other week, he was changing stuff.

Basically, Jim was killing his own business, both by not giving new things enough time to breathe, and by holding onto vendors and sources he was comfortable with who weren't giving him anything useful. That happens a lot—you're comfortable with somebody. Like, maybe it's a cousin. And they keep pushing you on the service and telling you it's going to be good, and you let them string you along.

So I said, "Here are the four we've got to get rid of today. You've had them for years; they haven't done a damn thing for you. I know a lot of them, and they don't do shit. Get rid of those."

Then I said, "Here are the leads I want you to get. Here's the marketing I want you to utilize. To do all this for a minimum of ninety days, you're going to need an assistant, so here's what I want you to pay them. So, I want you to do this for ninety days and I want you to believe these things are all going to work. I want you to replicate this with your entire team. Explain it to them and say, let's give it ninety days."

I also told him to stop talking to the manager he had. I said, "Why are you talking to your manager? He doesn't know anything. He doesn't sell anything. You already know more than he does. When he tries to get in your business, tell him to stay out of it. Stop talking to this dude."

We agreed to meet again in 90 days to see where he was. And he had his thoughts about what was working and what he wasn't sure of. But then I started showing him how everything had changed and what his trajectory was now. And at the end of that meeting we decided to keep everything. And in the next 15 months, Jim went from being a guy that nobody ever knew to one of the top five people at the company.

I'm not taking credit for all of his success, but I know for a fact that if he had kept doing what he was doing previously, he wouldn't have been successful.

## RESULTS AREN'T INSTANTANEOUS

If you have a plan for growth, and you're following that plan, you need to understand that you may have weeks, months, and quarters where you don't see any growth. You might have a year where you don't see growth. You may be doing everything right, but because of what is going on with other businesses, or in the economy, you may not see that growth today. You may not see results for three, six, or even nine months.

Conversely, the end result of any problems you have in how you're running your business may not show up for three, six, or nine months. When I evaluate a business, I meet with people and say, these things you're doing are going to be a problem. And they'll respond—yeah, but we're doing well.

But they just haven't seen the negative repercussions of what they're doing yet. And they will.

## TRACK EVERYTHING

You need to aim for 20% income growth year over year. If you're not seeing 20% growth financially every year, then something's not right with your plan.

If you're making $100,000 now, and in five years you're not making $250,000—if you don't see that trajectory—then it's time to reassess and make some changes.

Track your progress in a dashboard that shows you everything in one place. You can use Google Sheets or some other career tracker, but you absolutely need this to track your quarterly income, bonuses, commission, savings, and expenses. Keep everything automated, creating reminders to keep yourself in check so you don't waste any time.

You should also document the skills and responsibilities you've gained, plus the wins and losses you've had, such as closing your biggest deal ever, mentoring this many new hires, and attending or facilitating this many leadership training sessions.

Track when you last asked for a raise and when you should ask again. It's ironic that I have worked at companies where people have bitched, moaned, and complained about what they make, and I'll immediately say, when's the last time you talked to your manager or your supervisor about making more money? And often, they can't tell me.

Now, if the company's not making money, don't ask for more money. When I launched the insurance distribution, for the first three years, there wasn't anybody who worked for me as an employee who should have been asking for more money. We weren't making any money. But when we started making money, I made sure to reward the people who had contributed to our success.

Now, if you're running a business, you also need to track every damn aspect of your entire business. You should have access to all of that at your fingertips.

So, in life insurance, this would include how many leads people get for the day, for the week, for the month, for the quarter, for the year. How many sales they make for each of those time periods. What the profitability per sale was for each individual—the agent, the manager—and for the company. What are the daily expenses, and how much do they fluctuate?

For salespeople who are competitive, you want people to be able to see their numbers in real time. Salespeople want to know where they stand with everybody. They want to know if they're growing, if they're dying, if they're winning, if they're losing. And when you put that in writing, the peer pressure is the most powerful pressure in the world. You want everyone to see everyone's numbers.

In real estate, you would track your property manager's results. For each, it's how many vacancies do you have? What's your occupancy rate? What's your delinquency rate?

Track every single thing you spend money on and every dollar that comes in. Track profitability trends—are you becoming more profitable or less profitable? What are the impediments to your future profitability? Are leads slowing down? Is volume slowing down? Is profitability slowing down?

In your businesses, you won't see the negative or positive ramifications of all the things you do right away. You have to look at the numbers in real time. If you're just looking at money deposited in your bank account, you might think you're killing it, but those real-time numbers could tell you a very different story.

I come into industries all the time and ask, "How's everybody doing?" And they'll say, "We're selling this much per month." But when I ask the number they need to sell in a month to be profitable, they look at me like I'm crazy.

You need to have that number. Like, what do you spend on leads? What do you have to make in sales to break even? Nobody ever has the answer.

So then I'll spend 20 minutes doing the numbers. I'll tell them, "In your industry, with this expense, and this, and this, you've got to sell $15,000 a month. That's the bottom line. Everything below that, you lose money."

I track every single thing I can imagine. You should as well.

## GET A JOB WHERE YOUR PRODUCTIVITY MATTERS

A friend of mine worked as an attorney at a big law firm. He was working 80, 90, 100 hours a week, so I asked him what he made. He told me, and I said, that seems like a lot of work to make that kind of money.

So, he walked me through the equity program and buying in and all that, and I was like, yeah, I understand all that. But are there other firms that will pay you a lot more for doing what you're doing?

Because that big firm could get anybody over there. Lawyers just wanted to say that they worked there because it was a big, prestigious firm. It looked good to other lawyers. But he didn't have that firm recognition of being a partner, so they're paying him a low wage based on how much he was working and producing.

And I was like, what do you want? Do you want the recognition or the money? Do you want the good feeling, or do you want the good result? You've got to decide.

After probably two and a half years, he left to work at a really small boutique firm. Not an impressive office. Not downtown in the city where these other guys were. But the same exact work, the same hours, for maybe 200%, 250% more. He's been working there 11 years, and he's probably working less now than when he started. Same work, just a smaller firm.

Three times a year, he sends me a message—here's what my kids are doing because you pushed me to make this move. But it was his decision to go, not mine. I just made a suggestion.

If you're productive, you should be paid for that productivity. When I worked my job at UPS, I didn't like my hourly wage. But when I went to my manager, he said, "It's union-dictated; that's what you make." It didn't matter if I outworked and outperformed everybody there. They understood that I was their top performer because they tracked how long it took you to load and unload, but there was nothing that could be done about my pay. I could ask about it every single day, but that's just how it was.

I realized that I needed to get a job where my performance mattered. I needed to find a job where I would get paid more money when I helped the company make a boatload of money.

Whatever you're doing, you have to ask, am I getting paid properly for my level of productivity? And if you're not, you need to find the place that will pay you what you're worth.

## REGULARLY MEET WITH YOURSELF

This sounds crazy to people, but you need to have meetings with yourself at least every quarter. I tend to have them daily, but at the minimum, schedule a meeting with yourself every three months. Seriously, put it in your calendar so you don't avoid it.

Ask yourself questions. Did my income grow over the last three months? Did my role expand? Is my five-year trajectory on track? Document your answers, your next steps, and what, if anything, you're going to fix. If you're not on track, focus on identifying a problem and fixing it.

By having meetings with yourself, you're not tempted to just guess how things are going.

During the time when I got into the insurance business, I gained about 30 pounds. I knew I was gaining that weight, but I didn't get on a scale for five years because I didn't need to track it—my only focus was making money. Whether that was right or wrong, that was my focus, not losing weight. So, I didn't lose weight.

But once the company was in a better position, I realized that I needed to get in good shape and be healthy. So I started focusing on that. Lo and behold, I started losing weight and getting in better shape.

It's the same with money—you're not going to make changes unless you are tracking exactly what's going on. Even if you know you're not where you should be, if you don't know exactly how far off track you are, you're not putting yourself in the right position to change your trajectory. If you're five months from the end of the year and you're nowhere near your annual growth, you need that knowledge so you can pivot to plan B. And if you don't have a plan B, you'd better come up with one, whether that means switching companies, finding a higher position, or doing something else to make that growth a reality.

I was at UPS for two years before I created a plan B. That was when I realized—dude, you're never going to make more money no matter how hard you work. The guys who don't work at all make the same amount as you. You're never going to hit that 20% growth a year.

My plan B was to get into sales. At UPS, I was unloading trucks, thinking about life, thinking about what I wanted to do. That's the beautiful thing about unloading trucks—you get time to think. Unloading is pretty mindless.

I started looking at the management there, how much they were making, how hard they were working, how many hours they were putting in, how much freedom they didn't have. And I saw this wasn't a good path. I needed to get into sales.

While I was working, I was thinking about and creating my first plan B, which was to get a real estate license. I've had many plan Bs since, and many of those eventually became my plan A.

By continually tracking your progress and checking it against your goals, you will know whether you are on the right path or whether it might be time to check out other opportunities in your industry or beyond. Remember, if you are behind on your goals, taking risks and strategically shifting to somewhere else can make up lost ground in a big way.

→CHAPTER 11←

# REFLECTION QUESTIONS

1. Break It Down: Take your annual goal and divide it by twelve for months, then by four for weeks, then by seven for days. What do you need to hit daily?

2. Track Everything: Are you recording your progress? If not, start today. What gets measured gets done.

3. Plan B: If you're behind on your goals right now, what's your backup plan? Write it out.

CHAPTER 12

# PICK MENTORSHIP

## *FIND SOME, BECOME ONE*

Mentorship is essential if you want to succeed. Mentors can share knowledge that can shave years off your learning curve. They can help you avoid mistakes—including mistakes they have made themselves—and help you to find the hidden opportunities that are literally everywhere. They can push you harder than you would be pushed on your own.

There is value in both sides of mentorship—being a mentor or being a mentee. When you start, you will of course be a mentee, because you don't know a lot. But once you have built your skills and experience, you will be able to mentor others.

I've mentioned my first business mentor before—a guy named John Ellis who I first met when I joined a summer baseball league program called Niantic Legion. The Niantic team was very good, and you had to try out and show you were good enough to be on a team.

John Ellis became our coach. I knew him as a former Major League Baseball player who was now a successful real estate professional in our town. He owned properties all over eastern Connecticut.

When he came in as our coach, most of the guys complained that he was too hardcore. But I was like, this is what I need—this is exactly what I've been looking for. He was a tough SOB, and it was a great summer playing under him. I learned a lot about baseball. I learned a lot about life.

Now, he wasn't trying to mentor me. He didn't pull me aside and say, "Hey, Shawn, let me tell you a few things." He was very, very rigid. The nicest way I can say it is he was very old school. And I was drawn to that.

When the season was done, I was going off to college to play baseball, so that was the end of my time with the Niantic league.

And I said, "Hey, Coach, I got like a month before I go to college. Could I come work for you?"

Asking for a job is the easiest way to find your first mentor, because if a company is paying you to work there, then they're going to want to give you the skills to succeed in that job.

He said, "Doing what?" And I said, "Anything you want." It didn't matter to me. So he gave me a job working for his property management guys.

I really didn't see him a ton, but he was around, and I learned a lot by watching him—the way he interacted with people, the way he carried himself, the way he ran his companies financially.

And I was always picking the brains of the people who worked for him to figure out what he knew. They'd be like, "Dude, are you writing a book? You ask a lot of questions about Mr. Ellis." (They always called him Mr. Ellis.)

And I'd be like, "I'm just trying to understand the business model."

I think a lot of people were afraid to talk to him. A lot of folks are just afraid to talk to people and ask questions, but I always figure, what's the worst thing they can do?

What was he going to do, punch me in the face? All right, I've been punched in the face before. So what?

Was he going to cuss me out? I've been cussed out.

Was he going to say no? I've had people say no.

I really wanted to be around him and learn from him. It filled a void that I knew I had at that time as a young man.

I needed strong men around me to help guide me.

So I got a lot of mentoring from people just by watching them and asking questions.

For example, when I got into my real estate company, there was a guy named Frank who was a lot older than me. I saw how successful he was. I started watching him to see if he would talk to me. And when I knew I wanted to get into commercial real estate, I started picking his brain about moving from residential to commercial. And he advised me on doing that.

When I wanted to get into land development, there was a guy named John who was doing some land development. I didn't know anything about land development, but I had a lot of construction contacts that he didn't have, and I knew a lot about the town and the people there, and I had a real estate license.

So my early mentorships were created by leveraging and negotiating. When I got into life insurance, I met a guy named Jason who had been in the life insurance business for decades, and I knew I could deliver volume that made him want to help me.

Mentors will put a lot of time and energy into you when you're pulling in money for them.

I didn't care why someone wanted to mentor me—whether it was because they just wanted to help me out or because they'd make a profit from me. I just wanted the mentorship.

## BEING MENTORED

For the mentee, mentorship is a dynamic partnership where the mentee believes that the person giving them advice, information, and direction is qualified to do so.

You need to be able to articulate to yourself why you believe you're qualified. There are a lot of folks who seek out mentorship in the wrong places, looking for help from people who don't have the skill set they need. I often see people in sales seeking out mentorship from motivational speakers. I'll ask what makes that speaker qualified to mentor, and they'll say, "Well, I like the stuff he posts. He's motivating," and I'll ask, "Do you want mentorship in how to be motivated or how to be good at sales?"

Because while a motivational speaker might make you feel optimistic and positive, they can't actually offer you any advice or information specific to selling. They can't help you find sales opportunities or avoid common sales mistakes, because they have no experience in that.

If you are going to be spending your time, money, and resources on mentorship, you need someone who you can trust will take you in the right direction. Ask them questions about their experience. Make sure they've successfully done what you want to do. Make sure they have been where you are and know what comes next. Make sure they communicate in a way that makes sense to you—they might be great at what they do, but if they can't explain it to you, it's going to be an issue.

To be a good mentee, you need to have humility. I see a lot of folks who want that cheat code to get there faster, and when they meet people who have the information they need, they won't humble themselves and accept it. They just won't. And that is ridiculous, immature, and egotistical. Just acknowledge that you don't know everything and listen to the people who know more than you do. It's not that hard.

Most people's self-image is so low that they can't accept any kind of direction, clarification, or criticism. I decided to go the exact opposite way and be as open as possible.

It's funny that we have to modify "criticism" with "constructive." "Constructive criticism." If somebody is where you want to be, and they're giving you criticism and feedback, of course it's constructive. So why do we have to modify the word? Why should we say, "Do you mind if I give you some constructive criticism?"

I'm usually like, "Hey, Tom, do you want to get better?"

"Sure."

"So, you want me to tell you ways you can get better?"

"Yeah."

"Are you gonna get all offended if it's not what you want to hear?"

"No, man, I'm good."

"Cool. Do this and this and this. And stop doing that, bro—it's not working."

"Okay."

That's why I look for accountable people. They tend to have more humility. I don't mean they're meek and mild and humble. I mean they realize that they don't know everything and want to hear from people who know the things they don't know.

## MENTORING OTHERS

When I get good at something, I always think it's my obligation to reach back and help other people be good at it. Most people who have been mentored feel the same way—they want to pay it forward. Mentoring is, more than anything else, something you do because it's the right thing to do. People helped you. You help others. I hope in a few decades people are talking about me in the way I'm talking now about John and Frank and Jason.

Mentoring is also a way to grow. The more people that you can mentor and develop, the more you will grow your skill set in mentoring and developing.

From a business standpoint, you become powerful when you have the reputation of being a good mentor. People are thinking, *Man, working for that guy must be unbelievable—he's really helped all these people out.* I've mentored and developed so many others now that people look at me and go, "That guy can really help people." And that helps me in every business that I'm in.

There are so many reasons to mentor others. But the first question is—are you qualified?

When I was just getting into business, and I'd been in real estate for about six months, I remember a new agent saying, "I'd love for you to help me build my commercial real estate division. I see how unbelievably successful you've been in the period of time you've been here, and I understand you're the fastest growing agent in this organization across the country." And he went on and on, giving me all these accolades.

I asked whether he'd done any research before approaching me, and he said, "No, I just know everybody I talked to told me how great you're doing. And I've watched you with people, and you seem to be a really good salesman and good manager." And I said, "But why would you ask me? I don't have any commercial listings, and I haven't sold commercial property." I wasn't being rude or disrespectful about it. I was just saying, I can't help you, because I would just be making it up. It's not something I have expertise in.

Now, down the road of my real estate career, I became a lot more diversified in everything that I was listing, buying, and selling. But at that point in time, I just didn't know much about commercial real estate. A good mentor should be able to tell you where they can and cannot help you.

## WHAT I EXPECT FROM A MENTEE

For me, a good mentee is someone who takes initiative. They don't wait for instructions. They don't want their hand held. They don't want to be micromanaged.

Micromanagement is babysitting, not mentorship.

When I'm looking to mentor people, I want to know—Are you coachable? Can you take constructive feedback without ego? Are you obsessed with learning and actively seeking knowledge?

I want people who are grounded, humble, and willing to listen to the wisdom of others.

Are you resilient under pressure? Because every time it gets hard, I don't want to have to give you a motivational speech to convince you to keep going. You need to have internal motivation. I'm not so egotistical that I think I can keep you motivated seven days a week. And if I could, then you would just be using my motivation instead of your own. And then what? Will I have to spend the rest of my life motivating you?

I want somebody who takes ownership and does not make excuses. When I interview people, I ask, "Why did you leave that industry or that job?" And if they answer, "Nobody makes money there," which I've heard many times, I'll say, "You're telling me that there's an industry that's been around for hundreds of years and no one can make money at it? Does that make any sense? The question is, why were *you* not making money there?"

They might have a good answer. They might say, "Hey, I was capped. I worked my butt off for four years and couldn't get promoted." I've been there, so if that's how you see the problem, just say so. But don't give me an excuse like, "Nobody does well there," because that's never true. Someone is doing well there—it's just not you.

I want somebody with a very competitive edge, but not a toxic one. I see folks in business units that are pulling against people on their own team who can benefit their team's growth. That's the sort of toxic competitiveness I never want to see. I want you to have a competitive edge where you're like, "Hey, man, I hope everybody wins. I want me to win *more*, but I want everybody to win." Now, if you're in direct competition, you don't want them to win over you, but outside of that you should be cheering every time someone on your team succeeds.

For example, when I joined the real estate office, there were a couple hundred people that worked at the same company. We were all competing with each other.

Every single salesperson in that office was on the leaderboard. Every salesperson was vying for a bonus, and there were only one or two people who got a bonus. So we were competing, and I wanted to beat everybody.

That didn't mean I wanted everybody to lose—that wasn't going to make me better. I wanted them to win and challenge me. And then I wanted to win at a higher level.

The world is a big place—there's plenty of opportunity and room for everybody to win. So don't root for anyone to lose. Don't think that the only way for you to win is that everybody else has got to lose. That's pathetic. Cheer for everyone to win and challenge you. And then win bigger.

## HOW I MENTOR

Every mentor has their own way of doing things, but I'll just tell you my approach.

I keep it very high-level, giving them enough direction but letting them figure out the details. I love giving advice, but I know they're going to have to experience it for themselves. I show them all the land mines to avoid, and I watch what they do, but I don't micromanage anybody.

I'm blunt and constructive, challenging people without being discouraging. You can be direct and brutally honest while still being uplifting.

I offer blunt, real-world advice that includes my past mistakes. I share resources and recommendations of books and podcasts that can help. I give them real-life scenarios that push their thinking.

I encourage mentees to make decisions quickly. This journey is all about fast-tracking success, so making decisions quickly is a valuable skill even when the decisions are not absolutely perfect. Because the reason most people are not successful is not due to them making bad decisions; it's because they're so indecisive that they don't make any decision at all.

I lead by example, owning my own failures openly to create a no-bullshit, no-excuses culture. I stay humble, reminding my mentees that I'm also still constantly learning. I acknowledge their efforts and growth.

I also discover people's giftedness.

Every one of us has an area where we're gifted. That's the giftedness.

For example, I have an incredible work ethic. You'll probably never find anybody that works harder than me. That's a gift of mine—all the things in my life have combined to make me an unbelievably hard worker.

I also have the gift of a positive attitude no matter what's happening. And the ability and focus to learn things very quickly.

Those are some of my gifts. We all have a bunch of them. And it's important to figure out your giftedness.

Some people are really good connectors of people. If I see that, I'm like, you're such a great connector—why aren't you recruiting people and building a business? You're an unbelievable connector. That's what you should be focusing on.

A big part of being a mentor is helping somebody find where they're gifted so you can point them in the right direction. Because once they feel like they have an area where they're gifted, all of a sudden everything changes.

Some of your gifts will develop naturally, but you can also decide to develop a gift. I'm an unbelievably good salesperson—I was the top salesperson every place I've been. It's a gift I developed. Could you develop the gift to be a great salesperson? Absolutely. You just have to be willing to work hard at it.

You might have a gift that you think of as a flaw. Someone might say, "I'm just too empathetic with people, I listen to them talk too long, and I'm having a hard time selling."

Well, why are you so empathetic? I want them to be okay. Well, do you believe the product you're selling will make them okay or do better than okay? Yes, I do. Okay, then why don't we focus more on that?

So, one of my gifts is helping others identify, modify, develop, and eventually monetize their gifts.

If you can have a skill set, and you can teach it, and you can offer constructive criticism, then you can become a great mentor.

Ultimately, the key to being a great mentor—or a great mentee—is: Own your failures, stay humble, stay motivated, and live in your giftedness.

→CHAPTER 12←

# REFLECTION QUESTIONS

1. Find Your Mentor: Who's already doing what you want to do? How can you add value to them?

2. Check Your Humility: Next time someone gives you feedback, notice your reaction. Did you defend yourself—or actually listen?

3. Become the Mentor: Who's one step behind you that you could help? Reach out to them.

# CHAPTER 13

# PICK FREEDOM

## *OWN THE PROCESS, OR BE OWNED BY IT*

For my entire childhood, I watched my mother be owned by the process.

She was one of the hardest-working people I've ever seen in my life. She was smart and tough, but she was just a cog in the machine. She had multiple jobs and ran her life around her work schedule. She didn't advocate for herself to make extra money; she didn't ask for anything else. She just continued to show up when they told her to, and I think that she believed her lot in life was to work as many hours a week as she could to get by.

She never spent money on herself—she didn't have anything fancy, but she made sure that we didn't go without. She focused on her employment first because she needed to take care of me and my brother. She never said no. If there was an extra shift, she was there. I admire her so much for doing that, but she was completely owned by the process. If there was something that was happening in life, my mother had to defer to her job before she could make a decision. And I could see the men she worked for gave her no respect. They also saw her as a cog in the machine.

At a very young age, I understood that pretty much everybody I saw was owned by the process. And I thought to myself, *Man, why do people do that?*

While I was raised by my mom, I also saw how my father was living. He was a businessman, and it seemed like he made his own schedule. He had a freedom my mom never had. There were things that he did right and things he did wrong, but at the end of the day I saw that he was not owned by the process.

But my mom would drop me and my brother off at my grandparents' house, go to work, pick us up when she was done at two in the morning, drive us home, and do that day after day after day.

She worked so hard, and so I learned that hard work does not necessarily equal success. Was she able to pay her bills? Absolutely. Did she work hard to provide us with the things we needed? Absolutely. But it was always a struggle.

## OWN THE PROCESS

Every day, I think to myself, *Do I want to be a product of my environment, or do I want my environment to be a product of me?*

Your environment can be, and should be, a product of you. You are the only factor here—you decide. A no-days-off approach is easy if you decide to make it easy. When you listen to legends of winning and competitiveness, like Kobe Bryant and so many other people, you hear them talk about how many times they would hear other athletes say, "I know I've got another hour of reps, but I'm going to finish those tomorrow." And that's a slippery slope.

What I'm giving you in this book is my own process. You just need to work this process, and then you'll own the process instead of being owned by it.

I was owned by the process for more than 10 years. Even though I grew up watching the way people were owned by the process, and I knew I didn't want it, I had never really decided to implement a no-days-off approach with insane habits and consistency. And then one day I decided to develop the habits, consistency, and no-days-off approach that is what it takes to own the process.

You have to pick money. You have to commit to the grind. You have to look around at others owned by the process and remind yourself that you want to be different. When I was having tough times, working two or three jobs and feeling so tired, I would sometimes let doubt creep in. Can I do this? Is it achievable? But all I had to do was look around at people who were owned by the process and remind myself that I wanted to be different.

I wasn't born different. I wanted to be different. That's the struggle in today's world. Too many people believe that successful folks have something they don't have. But all they have is grit. I've helped thousands and thousands and thousands of people to own the process. They did it by developing the right habits, by being accountable, and just grinding away at it.

## NO ONE'S COMING TO SAVE YOU

I've heard people say many times, "I became an adult when I finally looked around and realized, ain't nobody coming to save me but me." I was hearing it from coaches when I was nine or ten—"Shawn, you become a man when you look around and realize the world isn't coming to save you. It's just you here as a human being. It is just you."

If that hasn't happened for you yet, then speed it up and make it happen. The sooner you acknowledge that and handle your business, the better off you're going to be in life. You need to accept the fact that it's you and only you.

Don't listen to people who are owned by the process. I decided when I was in my late teens that I wasn't going to take direction or be mentored by anyone who didn't own the process. And once I took ownership of the process and of my life, I saw there was nothing that anybody owned by the process could tell me about how to succeed. They can give me advice on whether a restaurant is any good, or what's a good place for a vacation. But once they start giving me advice about my life, there ain't no sound coming out of their mouth when they're talking.

Look, it's going to be lonely for a while, because most people are owned by the process, and they are never going to understand what you're doing. If you're looking for people to understand you, then do not decide to own the process. If you're looking for people to understand you, then do not quit your job and go somewhere else to make more money.

If you're looking for people who are owned by the process to understand you, then you shouldn't do any of the things I'm talking about. Everything you've read in the book—just leave it alone in that case. I hope you found it educational and entertaining, but nothing in it will work if you're going to be run by the opinions of others.

Keep your perspective, especially when you fall off. A lot of folks are good when it's good. I tell people all the time, "Don't talk about how good it is when things are good. Talk to me about how good you make it when things are bad—when the numbers say it's bad, and it looks like the world's caving in on you, and you can't even understand why it's going this way." Run your business and run your life in a way that people don't know if you're having your best day or your worst day ever.

## YOU CAN DO THIS, BECAUSE ANYBODY CAN DO THIS

My playbook has allowed me to make more money than I ever thought I'd make in my life. I never thought I'd be a millionaire, able to sell companies and make hundreds of millions of dollars. Never, ever did I think that was going to happen, because until I was in my late 20s, I didn't grasp that anybody could do this. I knew what had to be done, but I was still owned by the process, because I had that doubt. I thought, *Maybe that's just not who I am or where I come from. My family's never made any real money. We don't have any amazing pedigree. Look where we grew up. Look who we are. Look at the way people looked at us. Look at my family, across the board, and what they haven't accomplished.*

I finally internalized that truly anybody could do this.

I wasn't any smarter than you when I started. I've learned a lot about business since, but just believe, as you're reading or listening to this book, that anybody can be successful. Anybody can have the financial results they want. Anybody can grow their income 20% minimally every year. Anybody can become a millionaire.

As for those people who have become millionaires and think they have the market cornered because they're special, well, they're lying to themselves and everybody else. Don't play into their ego. Anybody can have the results they've had. I'm proof of that.

Now, will you do the work? Will you grind? Will you be coachable and teachable no matter how successful you become? Can you remain humble, even after you have achieved all of this success?

If you ever struggle with humility because you've done so well, just remember what I keep telling you—you are not special, and anyone could do what you've done if they just work hard enough. So how can you *not* be humble?

## EXCELLENCE IS THE CAPACITY TO TAKE PAIN

I became excellent by increasing my capacity to deal with pain and failure. To deal with the pain of being away from my family as I was building success. To deal with the pain of being told no, of struggling to pay the bills and make payroll, or dealing with unexpected circumstances in my life and my business.

If you can develop that capacity—to be willing to grind more than the person next to you, to seek out mentorship, to stay coachable and teachable, to work so hard that people around you say, "I don't understand what you're even doing. Why are you working like this? Do you think you're better than me?"—then you're onto something.

I tell the people talking behind my back, "I never said I was better than you—I just want more out of life than you do."

Don't apologize for wanting more out of life than everybody else. Don't apologize for wanting to own the process and not be owned by it. I promise you, if you will learn from the lessons I taught you in this book, and use the information I provided, then you can have this life.

Take no days off, develop the habit of commitment, track your goals, and you will have more success than you ever anticipated.

And if you can remain humble in spite of the success you have, and if you pay it forward to thousands of people who need help getting to where you are—then the sky is truly the limit.

## BECOME ADDICTED TO FREEDOM

I remember when my mom tried to get free by getting her real estate license. I remember her going to work. I remember the new dress and shoes she wore. I remember the Aqua Net—it seemed like in the '80s people would use like a half a can of hairspray every time they left the house. I remember how proud I was of my mom, and how excited, because while she was working her job, she was doing something else to allow herself to be free.

But it was a short career—I don't know if she even made a sale. One day, she just told me that she'd quit. Our neighbor, who was a mean old lady, said, "See? I told you not to try. It's not that easy." She was telling my mom, know your role and know your place.

My mom was always owned by the process—by her jobs, by her bosses, by her schedule. She never even got to retire—they fired her for absolutely no reason so they could hire somebody younger to do it for probably a fourth of what she was making. And from the day she started working to when she was let go from that very last job, the process owned her. She never owned any part of it.

It breaks my heart that my mother never got free. I wish she'd kept trying. She knew what it was like to stand in a store and realize she couldn't afford what her family needed. Did she ever think of just walking out with something expensive, the way I had when we needed that special baby formula? I wouldn't be surprised. That's what a lack of freedom does to us. I wish she'd pushed through the obstacles the way I have. I wish she'd found a mean old man to tell her, "Don't put your clients in control." I wish she'd had a chance to read this book and realize how achievable her dreams were.

Because when you start tasting freedom, seeing freedom, can articulate freedom, and can demonstrate freedom for your kids and people in your family, you'll be shocked what kind of habits and discipline you'll create to be free. You'll be shocked at the changes you're willing to make. When freedom is a guaranteed result, there's very little that feels like a sacrifice.

I'm thankful I chose freedom. That choice let me provide for my mom. She didn't have to worry about money or need to work again. She had a place to live for free.

Because I picked money, and I picked freedom.

When you become addicted to wanting that freedom for you and your family, you'll find your gift. You'll find your resilience. You'll find strength you didn't know you had.

Freedom is a phenomenal by-product of having money. And it's time for you to experience it as well.

Welcome to your life of owning the process.

→ CHAPTER 13 ←

# REFLECTION QUESTIONS

1. The Ownership Test: Look at this week's calendar. Write down how many hours you control and how many hours are controlled by someone else's demands.

2. Your Freedom Number: What annual income would let you own your time? Write it down, then calculate what monthly and weekly income that requires.

3. Your First Move: If nobody's coming to save you, what's the first thing you need to change this week to move toward freedom?

# ABOUT THE AUTHOR

Shawn Meaike is the founder and president of Family First Life. In late 2013, Shawn launched Family First Life, a multimillion-dollar independent marketing organization. Shawn describes it as "building a company that truly puts both the families of our clients and the families of our agents first." Over 37,000 licensed agents represent Family First Life in almost all 50 states marketing mortgage protection, final expense, life insurance, and annuities. Family First Life generated over $10 million in paid premiums during the first year of business, and the company reported $507 million in revenue in 2023. Prior to launching Family First Life, Shawn worked as an independent insurance agent, selling final expense and mortgage protection life insurance at a high level. Shawn earned an undergraduate degree in Applied Social Relationships and a master's degree in Criminal Justice Psychology, which led to a 13-year career in the Connecticut State Department of Children and Families. Shawn has successfully undertaken a diverse range of projects, encompassing residential, commercial, and land development. He has meticulously built an extensive real estate portfolio over 15 years through strategic planning and astute decision-making. Beyond his professional achievements, Shawn finds fulfillment in family life and resides in Boca Raton, Florida.